IUL ASAP

What People Say About Shirley Luu...

"Shirley Luu is a servant leader, and leader of leaders. She models the behavior she expects from her team. Shirley's ability to train and inspire people to greater heights is legendary. There is no one I would prefer leading me and my team than Shirley...till death do we part"

Dr. George C Fraser
Author, Speaker, Entrepreneur

"Shirley Luu is one of the smartest, hardest working, and most dedicated women in the financial industry. She truly cares about each family's financial security and independence."

Dr. Miluna Fausch
Pitch Perfect Executive Speaking

"Shirley illuminates the path that empowers every woman to generate her own wealth."

Tracy Lee-Anderson
Marketing Director, Women That Soar Media

"Shirley has more positive energy for helping people than anyone else I've known in my 40 years in this business."

Ron Wheeler
President, MKI Inc.

"Shirley Luu is a force of nature. There is no way to contain her passion for the financial services business. Shirley has been and will be a very inspirational part of our lives. We are beyond blessed to have crossed paths with this amazing woman who has brought enormous positive changes to our lives.

Victoria Le & Corey Vuu
Executive Field Chairman, FFS

"Shirley is truly a Dynamo in the financial services industry. Her uncompromising search for solutions to difficult problems, we all face, sets her apart from all other advisors."

Dave Greene
Executive Vice President, NIW

"Shirley Luu is one of the most focused and driven individuals I have ever known. Not only does the expertise of her craft rise above all others, so does the caring she displays for everyone she meets. If I am starting a financial team, Shirley is my first draft pick."

Michael Hardin
National Sales Manager, American National Ins. Co.

"Every conversation I've had with Shirley involves laughter and learning. Her story is amazing, and her desire and passion to help others find financial wellness and live their best life is truly inspiring."

Lisa Lickert
Owner, EMI Network

"Shirley's work ethic, tenacity and expertise regarding innovative financial products is unmatched. And yet, despite her success, she is one of the most trustworthy and caring mentors you will ever find."

Nicole Sparkman & Renee Brown
Managing Partners, Value Your Legacy Financial

"Shirley Luu is ON FIRE! Not only is Ms. Luu one of the most knowledgeable financial advisors that I've worked with, she's genuinely and personally concerned with me, her client and friend. Shirley Luu is a true one of a kind!"

Debby Montgomery Johnson
Founder, The Woman Behind the Smile, 501(c)3

Shirley's passion, compassion, integrity, energy and commitment to helping others through charitable outreach, financial education and her use of brilliant strategies to create financial security is amazing and inspiring! My daughters and I will always be indebted to Shirley in knowing that we will be financially secure in our elder years. Shirley is incredible!

Adonice Hereford
Mother of two

Shirley Luu has all the qualities of a champion: integrity, intelligence, energy and drive. But more importantly, she has turned adversity and struggle into a relentless passion to leave no stone unturned when it comes to helping people change their lives for the better

Phil Gerlicher
President & CEO, First Financial Security, Inc.

IUL ASAP

How to Win the Financial Game of Life,
Invest Like the Wealthy, and Generate
Tax-Free Income <u>with One 3-Letter Word</u>

SHIRLEY LUU

This book is intended to provide information that the author believes to be accurate, but it is sold with the understanding that neither the author, nor editors, nor the publisher is offering individualized advice specific to any individual's financial portfolio or individual financial needs or other financially related professional advice such as legal, tax, insurance, or accounting related. Seek professional advice when dealing with financial issues or when assessing the suitability of any product you may be considering. All illustrations and charts are for educational purposes only and should not be considered an endorsement or advice to acquire, liquidate, buy, or sell any specific financial product, insurance, or retirement/savings plan. Any data, statistics, or construed facts are presented with the author's belief they are accurate as of the date of this publication and in accord with the current applicable laws. As with any investment decision, past results do not guarantee future performance. Additionally, laws that govern securities and insurance products are subject to change and, therefore, any changes in law could render the information presented in this book as outdated or no longer accurate or applicable as it is currently presented in this book's edition. This book is not intended to serve as the basis for any financial decision or as a recommendation for a specific product or financial advisor. No warranty is made with respect to the accuracy or completeness of the information contained herein, and the author, editors, and publisher specifically disclaim any responsibility for any liability, loss, or risk, personal or otherwise, which is incurred as a consequence, directly or indirectly, of the use and application of any of the contents of this book.

 iKnowMyMoney
Publishing
iKnowMyMoney.com

For information about bulk purchase discounts, please contact bulk purchases, please contact books@iknowmymoney.com. To request public speaking appearances & virtual keynotes with Shirley Luu, contact: speakers@iknowmymoney.com

Cover Design, Interior Illustrations & Editing by Enzo Giovanni
Cover Photo by Ken Rochon

First publisher trade paperback edition May 2021

Manufactured in the United States of America

ISBN: 978-0-578-90705-5

Dedication

*To my clients – past, present, and future – who are like family,
to my team scattered all over America who are family,
and to my blood relatives who have no choice in the matter :)*

CONTENTS

"Don't look for the needle in the haystack. Just buy the haystack!"

JOHN C. BOGLE
Creator of the first index fund

1

FIRST THINGS FIRST

Hello, my name is Shirley Luu and I am *so excited* to share with you what has sort of become one of the best kept secrets in the financial industry. In fact, truth be told, many folks on *Wall Street* – especially the money manager types – simply do not want you to know about what I am about to teach you and expose in this book.

And that's because **you are about to learn about what I believe is the single, most powerful, financial security vehicle available for Americans today – the IUL.**

Now, I know that might sound like an exaggeration or hype, but I assure you it is not. This financial product could potentially completely transform your financial outlook – for life and beyond.

And while this 3-letter word has been one of the best kept secrets of the financial sector for some time now, the fact is also that the truth about what this type of financial account can do is starting to really 'get out there' as more and more savvy investors and families who have leveraged this particular asset are sharing the good news with their friends and peers.

On top of that, as more and more people like myself blog about it or talk about it on the internet or in the media (as I've done many times on radio and TV over the years), the good news about the financial power and potential of what this 3-letter-word can do continues to spread.

<u>My Why</u>

This isn't a novel or an autobiography so I will spare you the long-winded narrative on how I became me. That said, I do think it's relevant for you to know a little about my "*why*" - and it starts with a big financial mistake I made early in life that coincided with a major traumatic event. The theme of this after-school special is *I assumed* and let's just say that I wish I had taken the old adage to heart that "when you *assume* you make an *ass* out of *u* and *me*."

I *assumed* my husband had all of the finances in order. I *assumed* he would take care of me and the family forever. I *assumed* that nothing bad could ever happen to me. I *assumed* wrong.

As it turns out, life had a different plan in store for me. And that different plan revealed itself one ordinary <u>Wednesday</u> afternoon on a day that would end up being the worst day of my life.

It was the day that my husband died.

It happened very suddenly and it was a shock to my entire family, but here was the kicker – there was no life insurance when I thought there was. What?! Yep, that was my reality so when he passed on, I was left with no financial support, nothing, nada.

That's because little did I know that my husband had stopped paying the premiums on the life insurance policy four months prior to his death. This caused the policy to lapse and therefore, there was no death benefit for me to collect.

I have three children, but when all of this happened it was a matter of taking care of a 16-year-old daughter, 15-year-old son, and a 1-year-old baby girl. So, you can imagine the devastation I felt when I lost that financial support.

As a widowed mother of three dealing with my life being turned upside down, I soon experienced one of my lowest and most fearful moments in life. I was sitting inside a McDonalds with my three children as I was waiting to hear from the landlord on when I could move in.

And even though, thank God, we were moving into a new place as a way to 'start over,' I felt this dreadful feeling of homelessness and despair. I didn't really know where I was going, or where I was, or what the future held for me. I'm an optimist by nature, but doubts and fears were bubbling up inside of me in the form of questions I didn't have the answers to. Questions like: *how will I take care of my family now? How can I provide a standard of care that will be good enough? What if I can't make it work? What will life be like as a single mother? Where will we live and settle down?*

I may have seemed 'okay' to my children at the time, but

that was a show. inside of me I was crying. And that's because as my children and I were huddled up in a fast-food joint, I felt like it was a symbolic reflection of my new status in life. Is this how it was going to be now?

But in any event, I chose to rise up. Yes, my assumptions had cost me big time, but never again. What was my weakness - **financial ignorance** - would soon transform into my super power.

I didn't know that back then, of course, but now it's obvious to me. Now, I can see why things happened to me just the way they did. I *was meant to be a mover and a shaker, and not just that, but a messenger, too.* And now, ironically, I teach people all the time about how to not make the same mistakes I made.

After the death of my husband, I guess you could say that I felt like life was nudging me to do something more, if you know what I mean. Actually, forget the nudging. It was more like life pushing me off a cliff - and I was forced to either fly or die.

I chose to fly.

And that is when I decided to get into the financial industry. And I didn't just get into it - I thrived in it. And I'm blessed that I wake up every day knowing that I'm taking care of my family and that I get to do what I love the most - which is to teach people how to become financially secure.

So, here's the deal. If you are a woman reading this, listen up! Learn from my mistake and do not assume everything is in order just because your husband pays the bills. Do not completely detach yourself from basic awareness about your financial affairs, accounts, and your retirement savings.

And if you are a man, then listen up! If you happen to be the main source of income for your loved ones, you better have things in order when it comes to your finances and especially with regards to life insurance.

And if it's the woman who is in charge of the finances or the primary income producer of the family (hello, look at me), then you too need to make sure your finances are in order as well. And to the men in that situation, it is you who must not assume everything is fine and dandy.

❝ It was more like life pushing me off a cliff - and I was forced to either fly or die.

I chose to fly.❞

SHIRLEY LUU

Man or woman, bread winner or not, financial ignorance could cost you. And when it comes to your legacy, I'm sure the last thing you want to do is leave behind a financial burden on top of the grief that your loved ones will have to endure.

All of this is to say that my mission in life has clearly revealed itself to be to help people get financially well. That's why I sponsor the financial clubs at the local universities and colleges. That's why I teach financial literacy to churches and organizations. And that's why I train people on how to get into the financial services industry, itself. I want to empower people with the knowledge it takes to become financially secure and independent – that is my mission – and I've been on that train for over 20 years.

The Real Deal

The fact of the matter is that this 3-letter word is the real deal and it's making waves in the market – as in everybody *in the know* across the financial landscape is taking notice – and, if anything, is having to adapt to the very fact that this 3-letter word exists.

Why?

For the sheer fact that more and more people are demanding to have what this 3-letter word can provide. And when they can't get it in the traditional sense, guess what's happening? That's right. People are pulling large sums of cash and moving it into an IUL.

And yet, there's still a good chance you are one of the ones who still hasn't heard about the IUL yet or at least not until recently. And regardless of whether you have heard about it or not, unless you have an IUL yourself, it's highly probable you don't fully understand what the IUL is capable of providing from a financial planning point of view. I know this for a fact because every day I speak to intelligent, educated, professional folks from all walks of life who have never heard of or been truly made aware of the unique financial features and benefits of having an IUL.

On top of that, I know of plenty of professionals who work in financial services who don't know the full capabilities of an IUL – and that includes many of the supposed experts you see on TV. Therefore, it only makes sense then that most ordinary folks (not in the financial field) wouldn't have an adequate understanding or awareness of this product. ***The irony is that the IUL should be a mainstream option that everyone should know about.***

So, if you have been kept in the dark up to this point, don't worry – that won't do you any good now. Just rejoice and get excited! Because you are about to get fully briefed on what this 3-letter word can potentially do for you and your finances. And by the time you are done with this book, you will know what the other 99% don't fully understand yet.

And you will be better off for it – because at least then you will know what is possible. You will know how to leverage your money in ways that perhaps you thought not possible before. You will know how to do things with your money which the rich have been doing for many years.

What you are about to learn...

You are about to learn an alternative way to <u>save money</u> in a savvy way.

You are about to learn how to <u>grow your money</u> using gains in the financial markets while simultaneously protecting that same money from market losses (including market crashes).

You are about to learn how you can make your money last <u>for a long time</u> – as in a stream of supplemental income that can last practically for a lifetime.

You are about to learn how to <u>invest like the wealthy</u> and in a way that affords you unique tax advantages.

You are about to learn how you can <u>protect yourself</u> from sudden bankruptcy or financial disasters due to the sudden financial burdens that arise from unpredictable life events and traumas.

You are about to learn <u>an alternative way to save</u> for (as well as position yourself for) some of the biggest expenses that typically confront families, such as: college tuition, weddings, mortgage down payment, emergencies or home improvements.

You are about to learn about how you can instantly tap into <u>a 6 or 7 figure net-worth.</u>

You are about to learn <u>how to invest like a pro</u> on Wall Street without having to deal with all the complications and intricacies inherent to managing a stock portfolio or without having to invest ridiculous amounts of time studying the markets yourself or even without having the pressure of choosing the perfect financial advisor or firm to manage your money.

You are about to learn <u>how to leave the ultimate legacy</u> for yourself and your loved ones (or cause) while at the same time ensuring your passing doesn't cast an unnecessary burden on anyone else.

But here's my favorite… you are about to learn about how

to generate TAX-FREE INCOME FOR LIFE – as in a supplemental income stream you can "turn on" during retirement (or even before retirement) and have it last for as long as many years as you want or for the rest of your life, practically speaking, if you want.

You are about to learn how you can do all this and more with ONE financial instrument – I repeat – ONE financial instrument. That's why you need to read this book and pass it on because what you will learn in this book is something all Americans need to know about as soon as possible.

Knowing Your Options is Key

Said in another way, I'm about to teach you about an alternative way to save, grow, and protect your money – whether it be for your personal security, your kids, or retirement. I'm going to teach you about this option that you may not know of yet – and having options is the key.

In fact, it's my passionate opinion that you need to know that there are other sound, simple, and savvy ways to save, grow, and protect your money *in addition to* your typical savings plans such as 401(k), TSP, 403(b), Roth IRAs, and 529 Plans.

You need to know that there are a plethora of additional benefits and advantages that you can tap into if you have the right financial accounts. You need to know that there are alternatives – and I say that because often people feel the opposite. They feel like they don't have any options. *It's this way or the highway* or *get a 401(k) at your job or else*. It's those mindsets or feelings that people often express to me.

This is why on a very basic level all I really do for people who consult with me on a basic level is compare for them what they have now versus with what they could have with the same money. Here are the risks you have now compared with the risks you could have. Here are the protections you have now versus the protections you could have. I simply say, "hey, Mr. Jones, you have *this* which gives you *that*, but did you know you could also have *this over here* which would give you *that* plus *that* plus *that*?" In short, I teach people how to re-position their money if they feel it's advantageous to do so based upon an educated point-of-view.

In fact, when I sit down with prospective clients, one of the first things I do (after getting to know them) is I get to know their finances - their income, current savings (if any), investment and retirement accounts, current 401(k), IRAs, etc. - and I also make sure my clients get to know their own accounts as well (because I often find that they don't understand critical details about them).

It's important that you are aware of the realities of growth, risk, potential income, and longevity when it comes to your current financial accounts. In other words, you need to know how long your money will last. And if the reality of that answer makes you nervous, the good news is that there are ways to make it last essentially for the rest of your life. You need to know your money!

Notably, it's worth mentioning I'm a fiduciary as well, which means legally and technically speaking, I must have my client's best interests in mind when working with them and recommending any financial products to them. It's also worth mentioning that while I may work with them or deal with them all the time, I'm not a CPA or tax professional so while I may talk about taxes here and there, I'm simply trying to educate you on some basic concepts. You need to consult with your tax attorney or accountant when dealing with your taxes.

But again, it's all about knowing your options. Then, *and only then as far as I'm concerned*, will you be in a position to have a true choice.

I'm not talking to you about the choice you have in terms of whether or not to save money. You already know that you need to do that - and many of you are and have been doing it for some time now, but when you chose to save for retirement, your options were limited at the time.

That's why I simply want you to realize you have some real options now - and regardless of what you have done up to now. And given that it has become part of my mission in life to do so, I really want you to be empowered with this financial knowledge so that you may exercise your right to choose. I don't want you to merely have a choice of whether to save or not, **but rather I simply want you to know now that <u>you have a real choice on how</u> you can save, grow, and protect that money in a savvy way.**

Old Plan or New Plan?

What I often find as I review people's retirement accounts and money situations is that many people tend to have what I like to call the "old plan" as in an *old-fashioned* or *old school* retirement plan. The funny thing is that when I ask people what kind of retirement plan they have, they usually guess the old plan before having any idea of what the new one may be.

Now, there's nothing wrong if you still love music from the 1980s (*who doesn't get a kick out of 80s music?*), but when it comes to financial plans, if you are saving money exclusively based on plans developed during these times (such as the 401k which was created in 1978), then you need to wake up to the fact that things have evolved since then. Not only do we now have things like bitcoin and smart phones, but we also have retirement/savings plans that have evolved as well.

In fact, you could call the IUL the *iPhone of financial accounts*. It's not the best analogy, but like the iPhone, the IUL is a game changer, it's modern, and you can do a lot of things with it. But most importantly, the IUL developed organically out of natural selection - meaning it was developed by insurance companies in a competitive market. And whenever there is truly a competitive market, the consumer wins because the companies competing for your business are forced to develop better, more efficient and beneficial products that truly address the consumers' needs.

Again, that power of choice can only come if you know the right stuff which is one of the major reasons I wanted to write this book - so that you could learn about one of these choices - a real and viable option that may serve as a perfect alternative to what you feel compelled to do right now with your money - or at least some portion of it.

But here's the crazy part…. as it turns out, the choices I teach people about tend to be the most powerful and attractive choices that exist. It shouldn't be that way, but it is. And it's true because people are always telling me, "*I didn't know I could do this*" or "*why hasn't anyone told this to me before.*"

And the simple truth as to why nobody told you this before is simply because you have yet to come across somebody who knew about this particular option, this particular 3-letter word which is a true game changer in terms of its versatility and unique set of features and benefits that only this particular asset can provide.

Who is this book for?

I don't want you to waste your time reading a book that does not even potentially apply to you so let's clear that up right now in chapter one - in which case, if things look good, read on!

If you are about to retire or just retired, then this book is for you.

If you are recently married or married for years, then this book is for you.

If you are a millennial, gen z, gen x, or baby boomer, and wondering what are the best ways to save money, then this book is for you.

If you have a lot of cash on hand, then this book is for you.

If you have a high income, then this book is for you.

If you own Term Life Insurance, then this book is for you.

If you are currently employed and allocate money to either a 401(k), 529 plan, TSP, IRA, or Roth IRA every pay check, then this book is for you.

If you are looking for a simple, elegant solution to retirement planning, then this book is for you.

If you have a family or ever plan on having a family, then this book is for you.

If you are wanting to know how the rich have been saving money and creating wealth for decades, then this book is for you.

If you have a financial advisor, then this book is definitely for you because as I alluded to you earlier, many of the investor types on *Wall Street* are probably not happy you are reading this book right now - and that's because it could eventually mean that they get to manage less of your money in the future.

If you are an employer or business owner that truly cares about the financial well-being of your people and want to offer yet another savings option through paycheck deduction, then this book is for you.

And if you just came into or are about to come into an inheritance of some kind, then this book is for you.

If you consider yourself to be a savvy investor who's tuned into the financial markets and your portfolio, then this book is for you.

If you haven't started seriously saving yet, then this book is for you.

Most importantly, if you consider yourself to be financially illiterate or feel financially lost and feel like you have no idea what to do with your money or your savings, then this book is for you because reading this book will be a major step in avoiding the ignorance of what I think is the most dangerous thing to be ignorant about – your financial security.

Remember, I believe the financial instrument you are about to learn about is the single greatest and most powerful financial vehicle available to Americans today – so in that sense, I say – if you are someone living in America, then this book is for you.

Why listen to Shirley Luu?

You are about read a book that relates to one of the most important and sensitive topics in life – that is, your money and your finances – so it seems only fair to tell you a little about myself first.

For starters, I have been in the financial industry for nearly 25 years now - teaching people how to save, grow, and protect their money.

In that time, I have traveled all over the country (as I continue to do now) serving my clients, speaking at seminars, and doing live educational events. In fact, there is rarely a week in my life when I am not speaking to some business organization or religious congregation, or talking on TV or radio, or flying somewhere to speak at some conference or special gathering so that I may teach about the things I am going to teach you in this book. That all said, clearly, I'm doing a lot more *Zoom* these days if you know what I mean.

Admittedly, I am a bit of a workaholic, and those who know me would probably say that's an understatement. In fact, I am often called the "Energizer Bunny" because I just *keep going, and going, and going.*

But here's why that matters to you.

You see, I'm not just teaching every day, but I'm also always learning as well. I've got my ears on the ground. And even though I have thousands of agents that I manage, I also talk directly to clients every day. I talk to families and individuals. I talk to business owners. I talk to CEOs. I talk to really smart folks in the insurance industry. I talk to CFOs, HR people, and accountants. I talk to those who are about to retire as well as millennials - even to seniors in high school and college students who intern for my organization. I talk to average Joes who nobody knows and famous people, too. I talk to those who haven't saved a penny and to those who have millions in the bank.

The point is I am constantly hearing about everyone's

financial situations - the good, the bad, and the ugly. And in doing so, I have sharpened the saw so to speak to the point that after 20+ years, there is rarely a situation that I haven't seen before - which isn't to say that everyone is unique because they are - but the fact of the matter is many people are looking for the same thing and that's financial security.

I've also learned a few things here and there as well from the ones who were doing it right as well. All of this is to say I've practiced helping my clients develop plans to reach their financial goals for a while now and that is why I wanted to write this book - so that I can reach even more people and begin to educate you on something I believe you should be aware of.

And just so you know, IULs aren't the only thing I do or teach about. I'm a certified instructor in financial education that spans topics from budgeting to estate planning. And whether it's a simple IRA, annuity, term insurance for an individual, business, church, or union, I can and do help those folks as well. That all said, the IUL remains one of my secret weapons and most valuable assets that I often recommend a key asset for my clients as a means to help them establish a plan that provides a real foundation of financial security as well as the peace of mind that comes along with it.

Finally, while being a workaholic might be something I should balance out more in my personal life, the point is that it's a good thing for my clients - and for you - because the fact is I live, breathe, and *love what I do* every day, non-stop - and everybody who knows me will tell you the same thing. So, with all that being said, just know I'm about to teach you about some of my secret sauce in this book.

But Beware

Beware of the fact that I cannot officially recommend any financial product to you prior to knowing your financial situation. I also cannot give you any tax advice or recommendations on how to deal with your taxes as I mentioned earlier.

Simply remember that the point of this book is to empower you with knowledge and insight about this 3-letter word so that you can make an educated decision on whether you should take the next step and consult with an IUL broker so you may further inquire about its suitability for you and your situation. And of course, consult with your CPA, tax specialist, or accountant as well.

Beware of the haters who just love to hate as well. You know the type. They like to provide feedback even though they may not be aware of the intricacies of an IUL. Then all of a sudden, when they do *get it*, it's the best thing since sliced bread.

Beware of your own self-doubt. As you digest the book, you may begin to ask all kinds of questions to yourself, such as:

Why haven't I heard of this before? What's the catch? How does it work? Why hasn't my financial advisor told me about this? Why didn't my employer offer me this option? Why didn't my insurance broker or agent tell me about this?

These are all great questions and I intend to answer them all in this book. Just trust me for now when I say that IULs are legal, growing in popularity, and regulated by every state in America including the one you live in now.

Simply take the time to read this book and learn from it and in doing so, you will be in a much better position to engage in an intelligent conversation as you ask the right questions with the right people to determine what's best for you and your financial situation.

Beware of your financial advisor, too (*if you have one*). He or she may have the best of intentions, went to your wedding and is a good friend of yours, and yet still be unfairly dismissive of the IUL simply because he or she doesn't fully understand it. In fact, I would say the faster someone dismisses the product, the more you should seriously consider consulting with an IUL broker expert so you can get an adequate understanding of it first before you decide it's not for you.

I can't tell you the number of times I've had *know-it-alls* challenge or question me on the products that I promote - either in a boardroom or on a live radio broadcast - only for me to respond with logic, truth, and undisputed facts which they can't respond to.

The reality is that due to the nature of management fees on the securities side coupled with the fact that IULs are primarily sold through the insurance companies (*on the other side*), this means that if, for example, someone decided to move money from an asset managed account into an IUL, that's money moving out of *their* account and into someone else's account (i.e., *the insurance carrier's*) - so you can see how a financial advisor recommending an IUL could present a conflict of interest, depending upon what company he or she works for, licenses possessed, and/or the exclusivity to which they must only promote or sell certain types of financial products provided by their firm.

Beware of getting too excited, too. I want you to get excited, yes, but I don't want you to liquidate your entire portfolio overnight either. That said, diversifying your retirement plan is a crucial winning strategy for the financial game of life.

Simply put, when suitable, the IUL is a fantastic product and it seems only prudent that you become truly aware and knowledgeable about what this asset can potentially do for you and/or your family. You just might end up loving it and consider it the best thing since sliced bread and perfect for you, but first you need to understand it. That said, there's a reason why IUL accounts are growing at a faster and faster rate – and that's because the secret is out and the product is awesome.

2

NEW AMERICAN DREAM

I told you already who this book is for, but there is one special group of people that this book is especially written for. **This book is created for the people who are in the pursuit of the New American Dream.**

But to make this dream come true, it will require some *power* which is what this book is really all about – specifically, **money power.** And you need to get more of it. It's crucial to your health, to your self-esteem, to your overall well-being, and of course to your ability to deal with the financial challenges of life which exist for everybody.

But before I address the *New American Dream* and the money power it requires, let's talk about the *Old Dream* first.

The Old Dream

In a world full of dictators and government control of all kinds, coming to America has always represented a land opportunity built upon a fundamental idea that has attracted people from all over the world – that is, *independence.* For many, America represents a place where you can be what you want to be, and go as high as you want to go and are willing to work for – since what you put in you tend to get out.

Over time, while the heart of the American Dream has always been the pursuit of happiness and independence, what that American Dream looks like when manifested tends to conjure up various images when you think about it. The most classical version and vision of this American Dream typically features a *house*, aka your dream home.

Add some property in the front and back, topped with green, freshly-cut grass surrounded by a white-picket fence in a good neighborhood with good schools and you have before you the quintessential picturesque American Dream landscape.

Get that and as long as you have your 2.2 kids, golden retriever, and SUV, then voila! – you can check it off life's bucket list – *American Dream, check*!

To keep things simple though, **let me just define the classical (old) version of the American Dream as including the following: a) find a job, b) raise a family, and c) buying a home with a white picket fence.** Check those three boxes off the list and voila, your American Dream came true! *Or so we thought...*

Keep in mind that since the biggest purchase one typically makes in their lifetime is a home – and given that this feat traditionally implied that you had saved money up for many years so that you could finally pay the 20% down-payment on the list price – the purchase of a home was (and still is) considered a major achievement.

Then, of course, we had the real estate bubbled that popped in the 1990s due to the rise in real estate prices coupled with an easier home-buying process that featured no money down loans and putting people into homes that they really couldn't afford. It was only a matter of time before this dynamic would cause the housing market to burst as more and more mortgages went into default.

The saddest reality, however, during this time was the fact that as the housing market burst so did the American Dream for many people as well - as in many people lost their homes.

In a way you could say that there was a silver lining to all of this. The American Dream was flawed and that flaw was exposed. **The core principle of the American Dream was still sound - the pursuit of independence - but the ideal we were shooting for was missing something, something foundational.**

The American Dream should be solid enough that once fulfilled, you can't just pop it like a balloon. The American Dream should feel more how you would feel knowing your house was being built with bricks, rather than straw or sticks.

The New Dream

Fast forward to the year 2021 and the *Leave it to Beaver* reality of white picket fences and 9-5 jobs that you hold for 40 years so you can earn a pension - well, those days are over. **Eventually, you begin to realize that the American Dream is not what it used to be.** In fact, the utopian scene is much more fragmented now, more of a *Picasso* rather than a *Monet*.

You see, even if you were able to "buy" that dream home, the harsh reality of struggle to make ends meet continues. The rise of credit cards, higher education, and the pressure to keep up with the *Joneses* gives rise to more personal and crushing debt. Life is more complicated now. You used to have only a few major bills to worry about. Now you have countless subscriptions and micro-bills for things that we now deem to be *essential* to living life in the 21st century – like your *Netflix* or your *Amazon Prime* or God knows what else since everything seems to be "in the cloud" these days. In fact, most people wouldn't be able to rattle off all the monthly bills they do have if you asked them.

But on top of that, the big bills seem to have increased in number as well – from child day care to school and college tuition to nursing homes for the parents, special health care needs, etc. – the bills seem to just keep on coming.

And so, what's the result of all this? A harsh reality check – that's what.

All of these financial realities and stresses of life have given a big slap to the face to the classical American Dream. In other words, what we previously considered the ultimate attainment is no longer the supreme goal, and therefore, the classical American Dream is no longer valid. It's old – not old in a fine wine kind of way, but rather, more in a moldy bread kind of way.

It's no longer good enough to simply buy a home. I use that term, "buy," loosely, by the way, because we all know that buying a home really means for the most of us, taking on a mortgage – the greatest piece of debt you can muster up. In fact, for many people, the idea of buying a home is not even on the radar. It's not the main dream pursuit.

Furthermore, not everyone wants to live in a big house or start a family – so what about them? Is there no American Dream for them to pursue? Of course not. **That's why the American Dream needs to be redefined**. It needs to apply to everyone. It needs to (and has) evolved.

People have a lot more information at their disposal now and because of that they are smarter and more aware. Americans don't just want the façade of a dream anymore. We want the part that feels real. We want what's inside and underneath - we want the foundation. We want the part that makes us feel like we are tracking toward it rather than attaining the shell of a dream. **We want financial security.**

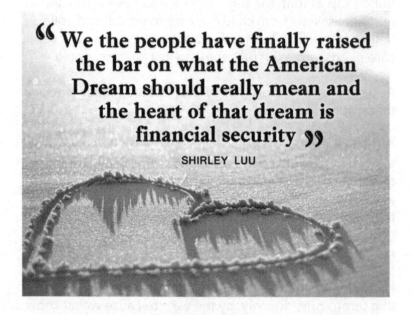

" We the people have finally raised the bar on what the American Dream should really mean and the heart of that dream is financial security "

SHIRLEY LUU

HIERARCHY OF FINANCIAL SECURITY NEEDS

From your school days, you may remember learning about **Maslow's Hierarchy of Needs** - a popular topic in psychology classes. It's usually illustrated as a triangle infographic with a hierarchy of levels. At the bottom are your basic human needs such as food and water. And at the top are your self-actualization needs dealing with personal fulfillment and living your dream life. In-between are other needs according to importance or priority.

Well, inspired by this Mr. Maslow, I've created my own hierarchy of needs – only in my version, I'm talking strictly about financial security.

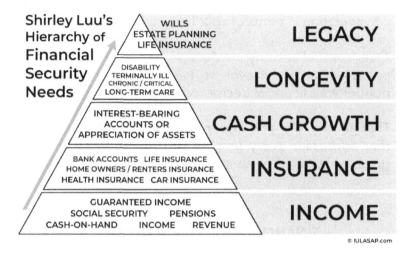

Shirley Luu's Hierarchy of Financial Security Needs

WILLS
ESTATE PLANNING
LIFE INSURANCE
LEGACY

DISABILITY
TERMINALLY ILL
CHRONIC / CRITICAL
LONG-TERM CARE
LONGEVITY

INTEREST-BEARING
ACCOUNTS OR
APPRECIATION OF ASSETS
CASH GROWTH

BANK ACCOUNTS LIFE INSURANCE
HOME OWNERS / RENTERS INSURANCE
HEALTH INSURANCE CAR INSURANCE
INSURANCE

GUARANTEED INCOME
SOCIAL SECURITY   PENSIONS
CASH-ON-HAND   INCOME   REVENUE
INCOME

© IULASAP.com

Cash-on-hand, of course, is the most basic of financial security needs, but it must come from somewhere (even if it's from a trust fund) – which is why **_income_ is essentially our most fundamental financial security need**. Any form of guaranteed income would also go here because guaranteed income represents the holy grail of financial security and provides a true bedrock for financial wellness.

As you ascend to higher levels of financial security, you get closer to self-actualization, financially speaking, which deals with your legacy.

Unfortunately, many Americans tend to focus only on cash-on-hand and 'money now', but that mindset tends to ignore protective measures such as insurance to guard you from risk (and bankruptcy) – or the need to grow your money in order to protect you from inflation as well as any interest charges that may be accruing against you on your loans or credit cards.

And then there's the consequences of life and death, itself, at the top which represent unique challenges and consideration in terms of your financial security.

True financial security involves making sure that you are prepared on every level, so keep this in mind as you ponder your financial decisions in life.

That all said, **did you know there's a financial product that addresses every level of this hierarchy?** Can you guess what it is? Yes, that's right – the IUL.

FINANCIAL SECURITY REDEFINED

The core concept of the American Dream will never change – and that is the pursuit of happiness and independence – but now people realize more than ever before that independence is not solely determined by whether you own a home or not. It's determined by your financial situation. Financial security is the *new dream*. **Financial security has become the new American Dream.**

It's true that, yes, the financial aspect was always there from the beginning in some sense. I mean how can you buy a home without a job, right? But now the end game is different. Now living in a house is no longer the ultimate reality we strive for because reality has set in and we realize that we still have to pay for that house every month.

Now, simply having a decent paying job is no longer good enough either. Now mom and dad work. Now we live in a gig economy. Now everybody seems to be trying to hustle for some side money when they can because multiple income streams are better than one. For some families, this is a must!

Even having a family, while priceless and wonderful, requires a deep sense of financial responsibility.

The point is just because you have a job, family, and/or a house in a gated community, that doesn't mean you've *made it* yet.

In the 20th century, people found a job and worked for the same company all their lives. In the 21st century, people have many jobs throughout life as they progress through various stages of life.

In the 20th century, pensions were a common thing. In the 21st century, they are more like relics found in a museum. Today, it's up to you, the individual, to set yourself up for retirement. If you don't have a pension, it's up to you to figure out how you can create one – which you can!

We the people have finally raised the bar on what the American Dream should really mean and the heart of that dream is *financial security* which can adapt to whatever vision or version you may imagine for yourself and/or your family.

Again, the feeling of independence will always remain at the heart of the American Dream, but now it seems clearer than ever before, that the American Dream corelates more to the degree you feel financially secure than any other factor in life.

Do you want to work at *McDonalds* or *Wal-Mart* when you are 75 years old? Probably not. If that's what you do to keep busy, then fine, but let it be by choice and not because you need to - and unfortunately the latter is usually the case. Usually, it's because no supplemental income was setup. It doesn't mean that he or she didn't earn an income working for many decades of their life. It just means they didn't place a small percentage of that money in a place that would allow their money to take care of them in the future. In other words, they did not plan to fail; they failed to plan.

© IULASAP.com

Essential Questions

This new dream puts the focus in the proper place and on the heart of the matter - the financial and money part. And as we shift into this higher awareness of what the new American Dream really is and focus more on the financial side of things, you will begin to ask yourself better questions, such as:

- What is the best way to take care of my family, financially?

- What is the best way to save my money?

- What is the best way to grow my money?

- What is the best way to protect my money?

- What is the best way to prepare for retirement?

- What's the simplest way to be smart with my money?

- What's the best way to prepare myself financially for emergencies or serious illness?

- Are there other ways to save for the future besides 401(k)s, TSPs, or traditional IRAs?

These are all good questions to begin asking yourself because it will put you in the right frame of mind to better filter out the infinite amount of financial information available to you as you seek out the answers to them.

The Million-Dollar Question

There is one particular question, however, that reigns supreme since it encapsulates all of the above - and that's why I call it *the million-dollar question,* and it's this:

What does financial security look like for me?

And making it more challenging is the fact that the answer is not the same for everyone.

The game, however, is the same for everyone in many ways and in the next chapter I'm going to talk to you about how you can win this game.

3

WINNING THE FINANCIAL GAME OF LIFE

Games. We all love them – from card games to board games to sporting games to puzzle games to video games to those addictive little app games we install on our smart phones. Regardless of age, race, nationality, or gender, everyone loves playing games of some kind.

And yet there is one game – a game of life – that most people are not playing nearly enough – or at least not enough to win. I'm speaking of <u>the financial game of life.</u>

You see, unlike most games which you can stop playing when you want to, the financial game of life is happening 24/7/365 – as in this game never stops, never sleeps, and never turns off.

Sure, you could say that 'at least when I die' the game is finally over, right? Not exactly.

Sadly, even then, after you have passed on, you still can't escape the financial game of life. Creditors will be knocking on doors since debts will still need to be paid off. Someone will still have to pay for the funeral and final expenses. And your assets will still need to be distributed via some legalized process involving multiple parties.

That's how gripping this game actually is.

Are you a Player or a Pawn?

The truth is if you live in a civilized society, you are a part of this game whether you like it or not. This is why I say that in terms of the financial game of life, you essentially have but two options: **to be a player or a pawn.**

If you are a conscious, proactive participant in this financial game of life, then you are what I would call *a player*. Players play games to reach new high scores. Players are the ones who get to make the moves and have fun. *Players play to win.* This is what makes you *a player*.

On the other hand, if you are an unconscious, inactive participant in this financial game of life (*whether it be by choice or by ignorance, it doesn't matter*) OR if you are a nonchalant, haphazard, or inconsistent participant – in both cases you are what I would call *a pawn*.

Pawns are manipulated and sacrificed. Pawns are a means to an end. Pawns are told where to go and are moved by others. Pawns are easily blocked. And just like in the game of chess, when a pawn is captured, it's considered to be no big deal – because pawns are simply not deemed as important as the other pieces on the board.

Not saving money at all or having an adequate amount of insurance is a pawn-like behavior. Not setting up your money for growth beyond inflation is pawn-like as well. *Shirley, how dare you call me a pawn!* Keep in mind, I'm not referring to your intelligence or kindness or achievements of the past or amazing potential for the future – I'm simply talking in terms of the financial game of life only.

Therefore, if you are currently saving money into a retirement account of some sort – like a 401(k), TSP, or traditional IRA – then kudos to you because you are clearly looking like a player.

However, I can't clink your glass and say, "cheers to your happy retirement" just yet. Remember, this is the financial game of life... and you don't want to just be a player – you want to *play* to win – but more on that later.

So, let me ask you a question then... what do you want to be in this financial game of life? A player or a pawn?

A player of course! Otherwise, you wouldn't be reading or listening to this book right now. Clearly, you are already a player. In fact, you probably already agree with me when I say that **financial wellness affects all aspects of our life,** don't you? This is why it's so important that we not only play this game, but that we play to win!

Now, if you do happen to feel like you've been a pawn more than you want to admit, don't feel too bad. Don't forget – I used to be a pawn as well. I sacrificed myself and because of my ignorance, complacency and dependency on my husband, it cost me big time. I didn't intentionally choose to forego life insurance as a critical asset when my husband died, but the financial game of life didn't care too much about that.

Ignorance is not bliss when it comes to the financial game of life. Ignorance will make you a pawn and eventually you will be sacrificed or captured *or* taken off the board – it's only a matter of time.

But don't forget. This poor little pawn (as in, *me*) who at one point was very much like one of those lifeless game pieces – toppled over and off to the side – as I sat inside a McDonalds with my children in utter despair and with no place to go – decided to get back up and get back into the game. You see, that's the one cool thing about the financial game of life. There's always a chance for a comeback.

And not only did I decide to come back and become a player – this little pawn became a Queen. And for my non-chess players out there, ***did you know that a pawn can transform into a Queen in the game of chess?*** You bet it can! That's what happens when a pawn reaches the other side - it can instantly become a Queen – which happens to be the most powerful piece on the board. And that's because a Queen can move in any direction and at any distance with a single move.

And now that's what I want to do for you – ***I want to help you reach the other side.*** I want to encourage you to become powerful Kings and Queens – masters of your own domain. I want you to renounce your role as a pawn in the financial game of life and relinquish your satisfaction for the status quo. I want you to take charge of your finances and become a proactive participant rather than merely a casual observer. I want you to be financially well and secure.

Frankly, you have no choice. The financial game of life is not a game you can ignore. Otherwise, the game will eat you up and spit you out and then step on you. Otherwise, you will be sacrificed by the game itself while the players around you continue to level up.

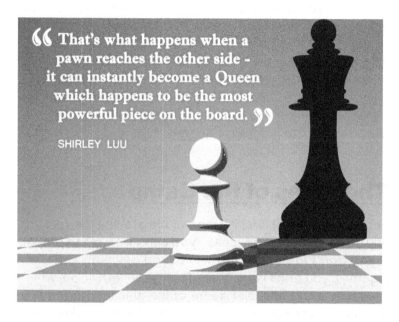

> **❝ That's what happens when a pawn reaches the other side - it can instantly become a Queen which happens to be the most powerful piece on the board. ❞**
>
> SHIRLEY LUU

So hopefully you are with me so far. Hopefully, you are ready to be a player. And if so, read on because now I'm going to talk to you about the game itself. You can't win the game unless you know how the game is played - so let's begin!

Object of the Game

The object of the game is to become financially secure. The degree to which you are able to satisfy this objective will be determined by how well you are able to optimize your current cash flow, savings, and investments.

The challenge in the beginning, however, will be defining

financial security and imagining what it looks like or feels like for you. **In fact, that's the million-dollar question: what does financial security mean for me?** Making things more difficult is the fact that financial security doesn't mean or look the same for everyone.

Said another way, the object of the game is for you to get to the other side - to that place where you feel financially well and secure, and to that point or financial state of being where you truly feel like you are the master of your own domain like kings and queens.

The Rules of the Game

The rules of the financial game of life are like the rules of any other game, in this sense - **you can't be a good player if you don't know the rules.** And you definitely can't win a game if you don't know the rules that govern it. So, when it comes to the financial game of life, this is where many people fail because they are too complacent not knowing the rules or too dependent upon someone else knowing the rules for them.

Also, the rules of the financial game of life are very much aligned with the real-world commonsense rules of life - many of which have become laws of society such as you can't steal or you can't cheat.

That all said, from a *player's* perspective, it's good to know the rules (or laws) very well for a few key strategic reasons:

1. **You want to know the rules very well <u>so you don't break the rules</u>** so you don't get in trouble. In the financial game of life, depending upon how and why you broke which rules, the consequences could be anything from

monetary fines to loss of privileges and rights to even going to jail.

2. You want to know the rules really well <u>so you know how far you can go</u> before you break the rules. There is nothing sinister about trying to maximize allowable contributions into an IRA account or waiting until the last day to pay a bill, right? Exactly.

3. You want to know the rules really well <u>so you can legally avoid the rules</u> if possible if you prefer it. Rules are rules and we need to follow them, but the fact of the matter is that depending upon what you are doing with your money, you may have different rules that apply to you at different times. Naturally, it makes sense to consider the rules you must comply with based on what you choose to do with your money.

4. You want to know the rules really well <u>so you can leverage the rules to your advantage</u> if possible. Not all rules are bad. Often, the rules will play to your favor, but only if you know how to apply it to your situation. In fact, one of the secrets to winning the financial game of life is making sure to leverage the rules of the game to your favor. Tax deductions are a good example. People are constantly throwing money away simply because they don't claim the deduction that they qualify for. Whether this is done by choice or not is another story.

Finally, there's one more key point to remember regarding the rules and it's this – don't forget that the rules sometimes *change*.

Which brings up another reason I wanted to write this book – **the fact of the matter is that the financial game has changed a lot in the last 20 years.** And, yet, it seems as if many (*if not most*) Americans, from millennials to baby boomers, are still playing the game by the old rules.

Game Piece

Even if you are assuming the role of player, you will still need a token or game piece or avatar. You are that avatar, of course. You are the game piece. You are also unique - and so is your financial situation which is like a fingerprint. And that's because your current state of financial affairs is based *not only* upon the various objective key facts and figures of your money and financials, but also upon subjective qualities related to your values, goals, and current situation in life.

FINANCIAL REALITY CHECKS

For example, take a look at the following list of *Financial Reality Checks*. These items of information (which are both objective and subjective in nature) represent key financial *states of being*. **These states of being or reality checks will surely factor into your financial affairs and decisions.**

Financial Reality Checks

    a) Your income
    b) Your expenses (cost of living)
    c) Your assets
    d) Your liabilities
    e) Your cash on hand
    f) Your savings and retirement investment accounts
    g) Your marital status
    h) Your personal and professional goals
    i) Your job, employer and/or field of work

j) Children status
k) Home owner status
l) Business owner status
m) Your family, dependents, and loved ones
n) Spousal support and opinions on all of the above

These reality checks essentially serve as *key inputs* that you will need to process (i.e., think about, consider, calculate) as you choose solutions for your financial security goals.

The Gameboard

When it comes to the gameboard of the financial game of life, this is where things start to get complicated - because you can forget about imagining a flat gameboard.

Think of it more as a virtual reality game.

This 3-dimensional limitless matrix consists of financial and legal systems, institutions, economic forces, and even math! Yes, even mathematical principles are involved. After all, this is the *financial* game of life.

FINANCIAL FORCES OF NATURE

Of the hundreds of financial "forces" you could potentially identify as being part of the game, I've come up with a top ten of what I believe to be some of the most significant ones that you need to consider:

Financial Forces of Nature

1. Financial Markets
2. Financial Products

3. Compound Interest
4. Risk
5. Taxes
6. Compliance
7. Inflation
8. Interest Charges
9. Longevity
10. Death

FINANCIAL MARKETS

Some of these financial forces of nature need to be harnessed like the sun for solar energy. The *financial markets* are one such example. Even though they are volatile and full of risk, the markets as a whole trend up and that is something that should be taken advantage of - which is why many of the wisest and successful entrepreneurs do exactly that.

FINANCIAL PRODUCTS

Financial products must also be utilized effectively. Financial products include things like bank accounts, savings accounts, credit cards, loans, payment apps, stocks, retirement accounts and insurance. It's practically impossible to successfully engage in society without using financial products. That said, some of these products are more powerful than others and others can certainly be riskier than others.

COMPOUND INTEREST

Perhaps most importantly, however, **in order to win the**

financial game of life, your money must take advantage of the mathematical principle known as compound interest. Albert Einstein called compound interest "the 8th wonder of the world." [1] That's saying something. The truth, unfortunately, is most people tend to underappreciate the power of compound interest. I'll get more into this concept later, but for now let me simply assert that it's so significant that if you don't take advantage of this powerful mathematical principle, you do so at your money's own peril.

RISK

On the flipside, there are other financial forces that need to be reined in so as to not let them get out of control. Risk is an example. With regards to some of the other financial forces on my list, clearly, we want to reign in risk. Risk includes all of the unpredictable yet often foreseeable possibilities and potential *for loss* – which may incur significant financial liability, expense, or monetary loss. This fact of life is what gave rise to the concept of insurance – which is designed to mitigate, reduce, or protect against risk.

TAXES

Obviously, it is wise to seek professional tax assistance when you can, but even then, you should always have a basic understanding of key issues that may determine the direction of your tax liabilities.

For example, *what are the advantages and disadvantages of using pre-tax money automatically deducted from a*

---

[1] GoodReads "Albert Einstein Quotable Quotes" goodreads.com (accessed May 24, 2021)

paycheck to fund a retirement account? Would you prefer to pay taxes now on the seed? Or pay taxes later on the harvest? Do your current investments owe taxes?

COMPLIANCE

These are key questions you should know the answers to – even if you have somebody doing your taxes – because the answers will also determine the type of compliance you must adhere to, as well. Compliance refers to all the rules, processes, fees, and actions you must take or not take **in order to comply**. Compliance is determined by your local and state governments as well as, of course, the IRS.

INFLATION

Inflation is like a tax on money itself before it even gets printed. Inflation is the reason that a soda doesn't cost a nickel at the vending machine anymore. And while you can't do much about it, nor is there any need for you to worry about it – you still need to recognize it and neutralize the effects of it. **How? Simply by saving or investing in a way that allows your money to <u>earn interest.</u>** Otherwise, your money will lose value with time.

INTEREST CHARGES

Interest can work for you such as with compound interest, but interest works against us as well in the form of **interest charges.** These interest charges are essentially a percentages game. You pay interest charges on your unpaid credit card balances, interest charges on your mortgage and college loans, and you have other interest charges that might not even be called "interest charges" like the **management fees** or **recordkeeping fees** that are deducted from your retirement investments. Either way, interest charges should always be minimized because the percentages add up.

Remember, when investing, you want compound interest, but when borrowing, you want simple interest.

LONGEVITY

Then, we have the financial force which is life, itself. But rather than call it "life", I like to use the word *"longevity"* because this puts you in the right frame of mind. **Most people want to live a long healthy life, but with that longevity we seek, there is a price to pay, literally.** In other words, there is a cost of living that must be considered.

For example, if you retire in your 60s and start withdrawing "x" amount from your savings every year, how long then will that money last? Until what age? How does the reality of that answer make you feel?

Do you have any supplemental income brewing for your retirement years? Yes, there's social security, but can you afford to depend on that? What if it's not enough to meet your needs or lifestyle?

DEATH

Finally, we have death. Death is something that nobody wants to talk about, and yet the fact remains that it is a *certainty*. And with that certainty comes the responsibility to ponder what would happen if you died. *Do you have a family or any dependents? What kind of legacy do you want to leave? How do you want to be remembered? Who* will pay for the funeral? How will your assets be distributed? Who will get what?

All of these questions must be answered, ideally, while you are still alive. If you don't plan, then there's a very real possibility that your family won't get what you feel they are entitled to. Don't let the state courts determine your family's assets.

This is why it's so important to consider these questions while you are fully capable of doing so and not incapacitated in any way. In other words, you want to ensure that you are playing the game and not the game playing you (as well as potentially your family). No matter what, these financial forces of nature must be reckoned with in order to win the financial game of life (see *Object of the Game*).

Winning the Game

Financial security will always be relative to each person and their situation. That said, regardless of who you are and how much you have saved up or your level of income, **the quest for financial security will always depend on how well you can <u>leverage</u> your money.**

Leverage is the key. Leverage is the secret to designing a winning game plan – which leads us to the million-dollar decision.

THE MILLION-DOLLAR DECISION

There are many decisions you need to make in the financial game of life, but in terms of leveraging your life's savings, there's one particular decision that matters most.

It's the million-dollar decision – and it's this:

<u>Where</u> do I <u>put</u> my money?

It's a million-dollar decision because this decision may literally determine whether you are able to save up a million-dollar nest egg or not - or whether or not you have a million dollars of protection – or in the case that you already have millions to play with, how you can minimize Uncle Sam's tax burden while making millions more.

And when I say "put my money" of course, I'm talking about positioning as in: where does your money reside or get sent off to?

LEVERAGING FINANCIAL PRODUCTS

It's your money so you can put it anywhere. You can stuff it into shoeboxes up in the attic or in a safe hidden behind the oil painting, but in terms of leveraging the financial markets, compound interest, as well as neutralizing some of the downward pressures caused by the other financial forces I spoke of earlier – like risk, death, and taxes – this is where financial products provide us a worthy option.

In fact, the choice of where to put your hard-earned money will typically translate to this:

Which financial products do I want to place my money in and use as my vehicle of leverage?

Financial products provide viable solutions to step toward your financial security by providing suitable destinations **for where you can <u>position</u> your money.**

When it comes to optimizing many of the financial forces I

spoke of earlier, utilizing financial products which are designed to do so, especially the ones that are multi-purpose in nature, are especially attractive.

Each product, of course, lends itself to a unique set of fixed and/or variable interest rates as well as varying degrees and scope of guarantees and cash accumulating potential.

And let's not forget the risk part. In addition to the management fees which subtract from your ROI, these financial products also come with varying degrees of assumed risk in terms of potential loss of invested money or principal. And you know how it is – the higher the potential reward or monetary gain, the higher the risk. And conversely, the lower the risk, the lower the gain.

So, when considering or comparing financial products and their potential impact on you and your financial security – simply look at it in terms of leverage. Ask yourself – how much leverage can I apply with money over here? What are all the features and benefits and tax implications with my money in this position versus that position?

In a way, you are trying to get more than what you put in – which is the whole point of leverage to begin with. A lever when long and strong enough and coupled with a fulcrum, will allow you to lift a weight many times greater than the actual effort expended – purely due to the dynamics of leverage at play.

Well, that's exactly what a well-designed and properly structured financial product should do for you, as well. It should leverage your money in a way that allows you to get a whole lot more with seemingly less. And by the way, to see what I think is one of the best examples of leverage in the market today, make sure to check out the **Bonus Chapter: The 5-Year(pay) Retirement Plan.**

Now, if any of that sounds too good to be true, then consider business loans and mortgage loans for a minute. These financial products are good examples of leverage at work. And it goes like this: if you can secure some money now, then you can use that money to generate much more money and asset value in the future.

FINANCIAL SECURITY WISH LIST

From financial reality checks to financial forces of nature to the positioning and leveraging of money, it's easy to feel lost while on your quest for financial security.

To help you get your bearings and simplify things a bit, I've created a **financial security check list** that you can use as one way to gauge the potential scope and value of a financial product you're considering. Think of it as a wish list of desirable financial benefits. Let's take a look.

Shirley Luu's Financial Security Check List

If I position my money into a(n) _____ account, it will be leveraged in the following ways: (check all that apply)

- ☐ *Supplemental income during retirement years*
- ☐ *Life Insurance for family*
- ☐ *Money in case you get sick*
- ☐ *Money for Retirement*
- ☐ *Money in case you die too soon*
- ☐ *Money in case you live too long*
- ☐ *Money for your loved ones because you care*
- ☐ *Money for your final expenses because you care*
- ☐ *Money that can grow (via the markets)*
- ☐ *Money for your kids' education*
- ☐ *Money you want to borrow if you need it*
- ☐ *Money that is protected from market losses*
- ☐ *Money that will grow*
- ☐ *Money that encourages you to save*
- ☐ *Money that is protected from taxes*
- ☐ *Money that's protected from creditors*
- ☐ *Money where my principal is protected*

GAME CHANGERS

Sometimes the game changes.

Sometimes, it's the rules of the game that change. And when this happens some strategies are no longer viable while other strategies are born, sometimes causing or inspiring new products and services. This is how the 401(k) was born - when a new tax law that paved the way for tax-deferred assets was passed in the 1970s.

Sometimes it's a new strategy that changes the game. Investing in the entire index was an investment strategy pioneered by John Bogle. It was a simple, but brilliant idea to invest in the whole market or, in other words, all the stocks of the market rather than trying to pick the winners and losers like traditional mutual fund managers.

And sometimes, it's a new financial product that changes the game. And that is exactly what the IUL has done to both the insurance industry and securities side - it has changed the game. And that is because this 3-letter word has raised the bar in terms of what's possible with a single financial account. The IUL has redefined what financial security should look like.

In fact, if you asked me if I had to rebuild my investment portfolio from scratch all over again, the first account I would begin with would be an IUL - and that would be an easy choice.

That doesn't mean I don't diversify or take advantage of 401(k) employee matching (if offered that as an employee). It does, however, highlight the implication of me choosing an IUL first - and it's that I'm using the IUL as the foundation for my financial security.

And that's because I can't get all the protections, potential market upsides, indexed strategy, principal protection, supplemental lifetime income options, monetary death benefit, legacy, and peace of mind with one financial product like I can with the IUL. It's that simple.

In fact, since I mentioned chess a little earlier let me do it again. The IUL would best be compared to the Queen chess piece. And that is because just like how the Queen can move in any direction as many spaces as you want in a single move, the IUL is highly flexible, scalable, and capable of providing numerous financial protections and cash accumulation features (if structured properly) with a single account and product.

Here's the part that surprises or confuses people. The IUL is a type of life insurance. Yep, it's true. In fact, the 3-letter word that this book is all about is a life insurance-based product, but don't think of it as only life insurance because you may miss out on the financial security it could provide you. This is not the kind of life insurance you have to die to enjoy. **This 3-letter word is a way to win at the financial game of life.**

And when it comes to financial products that are able to leverage the money-growing forces of nature while simultaneously protecting or mitigating against the money-sucking forces of nature, an asset class which has proven itself to be particularly instrumental to that cause is life insurance.

But here's the deal – today's life insurance doesn't operate like your grandfather's life insurance, and maybe not even like your father's life insurance. Today's life insurance products can do much more than they did just even 20 years ago.

In fact, much of the recent evolution in retirement accounts across the spectrum is partially due to the competitive pressure that life insurance companies have applied to the financial marketplace as a result of the innovative products they have introduced into the market.

In other words, as more and more people realize what their 401(k) can't do compared to what this life insurance product 'over there' can do, more people are moving large amounts of cash from their traditional retirement accounts into these life insurance policies which provide them with many of the same financial benefits, plus more.

If that is a real trend (which it is), then there has to be good reasons for it (and there are).

Also, when I say that life insurance doesn't operate like your dad's or granddad's life insurance what am I implying? That the rules have changed. And as it turns out, in the life insurance part of the game, the rules have changed in a dramatic way that benefits the consumer.

This is why when I sit down with potential clients I often talk about the **old plans vs. the new plans**. I explain it this way because it emphasizes the point that today's life insurance products are modern, evolutionary versions that are significantly different from the old-fashioned varieties such as term or whole life that you are accustomed to think about when you think of life insurance.

On the contrary, based on today's rules, it is my opinion as I told you from the onset – that the I.U.L is the single, most powerful, financial security vehicle available for Americans today. And in the next few chapters I'm going to explain to you all about this amazing 3-letter word.

4

LIFE 101

Leveraging life insurance effectively has been a winning move in the financial game of life practically since its existence.

In fact, *did you know that Walt Disney famously used life insurance to ultimately get the money he needed to build Disney World?* [2]

Or that Ray Kroc used his life insurance in the early days of McDonalds to get things going, as well? [3]

In both these cases, life insurance was utilized as an asset to borrow money against. Think about that. Nobody died, and yet the cash values within these permanent policies were leveraged to keep two of the most iconic companies afloat long enough for them to grow into the empires they

---

[2] John Hutchinson "Famous Entrepreneurs Who Used Whole Life Insurance as their own Bank" bankingtruths.com (accessed May 24, 2021)
[3] John Hutchinson "Famous Entrepreneurs Who Used Whole Life Insurance as their own Bank" bankingtruths.com (accessed May 24, 2021)

are today.

And then there's the personal side of life insurance - which is quite magical when you think about it...

Simply ponder the magnitude of personal financial protection you get the moment you successfully secure a life insurance policy. On that day, for a fraction of the cost, you are suddenly worth hundreds of thousands of dollars if not millions, simply by utilizing one of the best leveraging financial products created by civilized society - life insurance!

But again, not all life insurance, even permanent, is created equal, which is why you always need to make sure that you are working with a licensed professional who really knows how to play this game.

Now I know what you might be thinking... *Shirley, just tell me about the IUL!*

I hear you, but to better understand and appreciate the IUL, you need to have a fundamental understanding of how life insurance generally works, first.

That's why I want to do a quick rudimentary crash course on life insurance which will be a helpful foundation as we do our deep dive into the world of IULs in the next few chapters.

Don't you go off and run now! This is important stuff and everyone should have some financial literacy and basic understanding on how life insurance works - and that's because **it plays a major role in winning the financial game of life!**

What is life insurance?

Traditionally speaking, life insurance offers financial protection in the form of a lump sum payment (called the "**death benefit**") that is paid from the **insurance company** to the **beneficiary(ies)** listed in the contract (or "**policy**") when the person covered by the policy (the "**insured**") dies.

In exchange for this financial death benefit, you as the "**policy owner**," make payments to the insurance company as per the contract terms. These payments are called "**premiums**." These premium payments are what keep the policy contract "**in force**" (as in *active and in good standing*). If, however, you do not pay the premiums according to the contract, you run the risk of a "**policy lapse**" in which case your policy may be considered null and void and would, therefore, cease to offer any financial protection or death benefit whatsoever.

Why people buy life insurance?

Life insurance provides significant financial protection (in terms of monetary compensation) against the various financial burdens and pressures that arise for you or your loved ones when people die. Being unprepared to deal with the financial responsibilities that result when our loved ones or spouses die could leave you in dire straits very quickly.

More specifically, there are a bunch of reasons why people buy life insurance – and I would know because I've been in the industry for 20+ years!

Here are some common ones below:

Reasons People Buy Life Insurance

- As mortgage protection
- As income protection (for your loved ones)
- Having Cash Value so when I need it
- Pass on money to family (leaving inheritance)
- As debt (extra burden) protection
- As funeral expense protection

In terms of the "why," the fundamental root logic for the existence of life insurance is that **the death benefit replaces the lost income caused by the death of the insured**. Naturally, those that would have benefitted from the continual financial support of the insured are the ones usually selected to as the beneficiaries of the life insurance contract. That said, whoever owns the life insurance policy is the one who determines the beneficiaries.

So, for example, if a 40-year-old married father of three were to suddenly die, his family would miss out on about

25 years of potential income that he would have theoretically earned had he stayed alive. Life insurance, therefore, is a solution to protect against that financial loss.

It's a great concept actually which is why life insurance is a critical component to true financial security -- especially if you have a family. That said, even if you don't have a family in the traditional sense, you may still value leaving a legacy for extended family, covering your own funeral and final expenses, or for other non-profit reasons and causes.

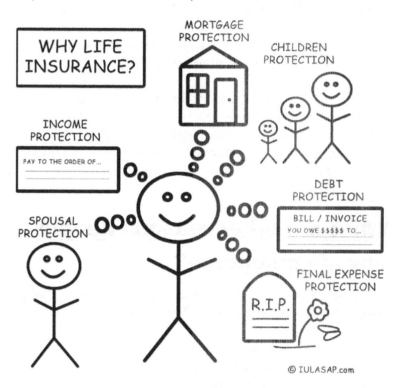

© IULASAP.com

How much life insurance?

In terms of *how much life insurance* you may need (as in,

how much death benefit compensation), that depends on a bunch of personal and financial factors such as your financial needs, income, lifestyle, family members, etc., but for the moment, let's think about it purely from a mortgage protection point of view as an example...

If you had a family and just took on a **30-year home mortgage** that was **$1500/mo.** that you were financially responsible for as the primary income producer (a.k.a. the bread winner), then you would **multiply $1500 x 12 (months) x 30 (years) to get $540,000**. This amount equals the minimal amount of life insurance you would need to cover the mortgage payments so that your family would still have and keep their home.

Keep in mind that in this scenario the $540k theoretically only covers the mortgage payments. After assessing your financial needs and situation, you may conclude that you need 2 to 3 times that amount. It all depends, of course, on your situation and goals.

What are other reasons people buy life insurance?

There are, however, some other common reasons why people buy life insurance as well such as:

- You get a raise (lifestyle change)
- Protecting a business (like keyman insurance)
- As parental protection
- As sibling protection
- College funding
- Leverage in cases of seeking loans
- Need More Living Benefits

- As grandchildren protection
- As social security protection
- For protecting your business (key-man insurance)
- Cash Accumulation for Retirement
- Additional Long-term care financial support

A new job, raise, or any other significant increase in income would suggest an increase in lifestyle expenses as well. In other words, the amount of money that used to cover your monthly expenses has increased. Therefore, if your life insurance was configured to account for a lifestyle that no longer applies, you may need to revisit your numbers.

As we get older so do our parents (as well as our other family members) so depending upon their degree of independence and financial stability, you may end up having to bear some of the financial burden to take care of them down the road. This is especially true if/when long-term care is needed. And God forbid, if someone were to become critically ill or diagnosed with some type of terminal illness, you may end up having to make some very difficult financial decisions regarding health care.

The good news is that there are life insurance protections that exist for cases like these called **living benefits** - *which* can provide you additional financial support right when you need it most. In other words, someone doesn't have to die in order for you to receive money!

Finally, with regards to social security, people have all kinds of opinions on whether these funds will actually exist when they need it, but let's assume those funds are fully intact. The first question you have to ask yourself is whether or not you would even qualify for social security? Generally speaking, you had to have worked and contributed into the "system" for a prerequisite number of years before you can. There are some exceptions to this rule, especially with regards to spouses, but even then, can you afford to live only on social security? And did you know that you can actually become disqualified from receiving social security as well?

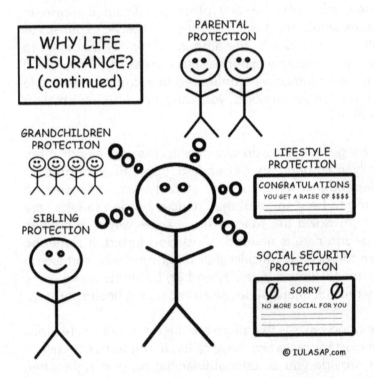

There are more reasons why people choose to get life insurance (especially with regards to the IUL), but we'll save those for the next chapter. In the meantime, let's continue with our Life 101 review.

Life insurance lasts how long?

There are two major branches of life insurance –

determined by how long (in terms of time) a policy is designed to protect the insured for. They are:

1. **Temporary Life Insurance**
2. **Permanent Life Insurance**

Temporary life insurance, better known as "**term life insurance**" protects you for a temporary amount of time. It could be 15, 20, 25, or 30 years.

With term life insurance, the insurance company may or may not end up paying the death benefit established in the policy contract. It all depends on when you die. For example, if you happen to win this twisted hedged bet on your life and you die within the covered window of time, then yes, the death benefit (monetary compensation) would be paid to your designated beneficiary(ies) (assuming the policy was in force at the time of death, of course).

However, if you lose this hedge and you live past the end point of the contractual term indicated within the policy (even just by one day), then the life insurance company has fulfilled its contractual obligation and served its purpose, and therefore, no longer owes you any death benefit protection. At this point, if you wanted to continue coverage, you would have to buy more life insurance.

Why is this a big deal?

Because if you had a 30-year non-renewable term life insurance and it just expired, you are now 30 years older and **the cost of life insurance will increase dramatically for you by as much as hundreds of dollars per month.**

Notably, most of the commercials I see on TV promoting

life insurance is selling term life insurance.

The 2 Major Types of Life Insurance

PERMANENT PROTECTION (to 100 yrs old and beyond)

TEMPORARY PROTECTION (until 65 yrs.old)

35 years old

© IULASAP.com

On the other hand, permanent life insurance covers you for your entire life (or technically speaking, often up to 120 years old). So, if you had this kind of policy, assuming the policy is in force, the insurance company would definitely pay a death benefit at some point to your designated beneficiaries whenever you pass on.

A popular and well-known type of permanent life insurance is called whole life. The good news here is that, unlike term insurance, **whole life policies have cash value** and typically offer fixed interest rates in the neighborhood of 4% per year.

How do I get life insurance?

Typically, life insurance is sold via **state licensed agents** who have been appointed by a carrier to sell their line of life insurance products. Life insurance products are regulated by both state and federal agencies.

It is common to come across agents who only sell insurance products exclusively from one company – which is, therefore, considered a **captive agency**.

Sometimes, financial service professionals like myself, are not restricted to sell only one type of product or exclusively from one company – and are free to broker life insurance products in the best interests of the client as we see fit from the vast array of life insurance companies and products that exist. Companies which sell financial products and insurance in this manner are considered **non-captive agencies.** In fact, I often tell my prospective clients, ***"I am a non-captive agency"*** because I think that it is a key distinction my prospective clients should know.

LIFE INSURANCE VIA BROKER AGENT

Naturally, I think the consumer is better off dealing with a **broker agent** such as myself that is free to choose from a variety of product lines AND from a variety of reputable A-rated companies that fits the financial plan, needs, and best interests of the client.

It's also worth mentioning that there are a plethora of life insurance companies competing for your business. This dynamic benefits you the consumer and keeps the carriers on their toes as they constantly refine their products to stay competitive. On top of that, as a broker agent who has thousands of agents in my organization and under my wing, I sometimes have the leverage to negotiate even better terms (than are publicly promoted) for particular financial products - which then become exclusively available for the clients of my entire organization.

What's the process like?

Usually (and preferably), the agent should begin by getting to know you and your financial situation in order to best assess your needs, desires, and best interests.

Expect to provide some basic financial information about yourself such as your current income, savings, investments, marital status, home ownership status, etc. This information is not required necessarily to get life insurance per se; it just helps the professional you are dealing with to better advise you. The more detail you can provide about your financial and personal situation, the better the recommendation you will received.

Then, of course, there are the specific types of protection or financial features you may be seeking such as mortgage protection or cash value.

Eventually, the agent should provide you a summary report of some kind that essentially breaks down the key guarantees or features of a recommended product as well as any other product literature if it exists. When dealing with products that provide cash accumulation based on various interest rates and algorithmic values, you should definitely see some type of ***illustration*** - a hypothetical forecast report that shows various account values at different time intervals under hypothetical market conditions so you can see how your money would grow and develop with time.

For certain insurance products and depending on various factors such as your age, last medical checkup, or other things, you may have to go through what's called ***medical underwriting***.

Medical underwriting is basically an additional step (which is quite typical) to the process of getting life insurance depending on the kind of life insurance you are getting and how it's structured. They do this in order to determine if you will be offered a contract, number one... and also to classify you into one of their main risk categories. Generally speaking, the healthier and younger you are, the better rating you will get which means your cost of insurance will be slightly lower than those assigned to the higher risk categories.

The good news is that medical underwriting is OFTEN NOT REQUIRED to get approved for a life insurance policy - even for permanent 7-figure policies. The reason it's not required is that insurance companies have access to restricted database information through what's called the MIB (Medical Insurance Bureau). Similar to how credit score companies know your credit report, the MIB has access to your medical history.

There is also something called guaranteed issue policies, which as the name implies are policies you are guaranteed to be approved for regardless of health condition, but just keep in mind these policies tend to be much more costly and tend to be optimized to serve group plans.

After you have selected your product and the agent has structured it to your liking and you are passed the medical underwriting (if it was necessary), the insurance company will process all your info and eventually either offer you a **policy contract** or not. If they do, you then have a period of time to review it, sign it, and pay your first premium. At that point, voilà, you have life insurance!

How does life insurance differ?

While I just gave you a super simple review of life insurance, why it exists, and how you can get it, it's important to understand how and why life insurance differs from plan to plan.

The first major differentiator is as I told you already is the length of protection – as in temporary or permanent. There are some other key differentiators worth mentioning as well, however, because at the end of the day, the quality of your plan and how well it's optimized to suit your financial needs will probably be determined by the following:

- *The life insurance carrier* of the product
- *The agent* you are dealing with
- *The standard provisions* of your plan or policy
- *The additional provisions* you choose to add
- How the agent structures and designs your plan
- The premium you can afford
- Retirement Component

The Difference Makers For Your Plan

AGENT — BROKER AGENT

Since 1805 — Life Insurace Company

PLAN STRUCTURE (AGENT CONFIGURATION) — x-X=

RIDERS — EXTRA

PROVISIONS — POLICY CONTRACT

© IULASAP.con

Regardless of who assists you in the process of getting life insurance, it's important to remember that the **contract** (or **policy** or **plan**) you end up with is ultimately between you and the life insurance company - and not the agent or broker agent that facilitated the process. For this reason, it's important that the company that provides you the policy is reputable and has a good rating.

Furthermore, another key element to this elixir we call life insurance is the contract itself, namely the set of **provisions** that come with and are unique to the product which you are getting. These provisions are clauses in the contract that define the terms for specific features and benefits of your policy.

There are additional provisions known as **riders** which you may be able to opt-in to depending upon the nature of the financial product you are dealing with. These riders usually add to or alter your coverage or plan in some significant way – sometimes acting as the **bells and whistles** of the plan. In short, these riders tend to act as upgrades, and while some are free, they tend to add to the cost of insurance, and therefore, the premium you pay. This is because these riders tend to add more cost or risk to the insurance company.

For example, a very popular rider that may or may not come standard with a life insurance policy is the **accelerated death benefit rider.** This rider is essentially responsible for living benefits which allows you to tap into death benefit money while you are still alive if certain conditions are met as per the contract. These conditions are related to cases of critical, chronic, and terminal illness which when triggered allows you to tap into your death benefit for extra financial support while you need it.

How do I find a broker agent?

I have personally trained thousands of people in the fields of life insurance and financial services. In fact, I have licensed financial services specialists located throughout the country *and in every state* – so in case you are looking for someone that was trained by me (or perhaps even me myself, simply go to **https://iulasap.com/agent** to find a state licensed agent. Whether you are looking for temporary or permanent life insurance or other financial services, I or someone on my team will take great care of you.

Now you are ready.

Now that you have a basic understanding of life insurance, you are ready to learn about the *three-letter word* that could end up becoming your most beloved asset when it comes to your peace of mind and financial security.

I am, of course, referring to the IUL. And now you are about to learn all about it.

5

THE 3-LETTER WORD EXPLAINED

I've already talked to you about what I believe is the **new American dream** – which is to have financial security.

And that this quest for financial security **is like a game** in which you must strive to be a player that seeks to win this game. Otherwise, the game will treat you like a pawn.

And finally, that **leveraging life insurance** is a proven strategy to win this financial game of life.

But now I'm going to finally explain to you all about my **secret weapon** that I often use to apply this winning strategy – which is the three-letter word that this book is all about, of course. In fact, it's one of my favorite ways to help clients leap toward their financial security and win the game of life, save money, and generate a tax-free supplemental income stream during retirement.

That three-letter word is IUL -- pronounced one letter at a time as an acronym -- and in just a minute, I'm going to list **MY TOP 12 REASONS** why I believe the IUL makes a worthy cornerstone for your financial security.

Wikipedia.com defines cornerstone as *"the first stone set in the construction of a masonry foundation. All other stones will be set in reference to this stone, thus determining the position of the entire structure."*

And this is why you will often hear me say "cornerstone" as I refer to the IUL and that's **because the IUL is potentially a great foundational piece to the puzzle you are trying to solve regarding your financial security.**

What is IUL?

The IUL is an insurance-based financial product that you typically setup through the assistance of a state licensed financial services professional or agent who must conduct themselves as a **fiduciary** – and, therefore, act in the best interests of the client.

What does IUL stand for?

IUL is an acronym that stands for **Indexed Universal Life.** Sometimes, you may simply see the word "index" instead without the "ed" at the end.

Indexed refers to the manner by which cash accumulation is credited within an IUL -- which is primarily based upon the growth performance of one or more financial markets (index or indices) such as the *Dow Jones* or *S&P 500*.

The word **universal** refers to the flexibility and multi-purpose nature for which an IUL can be customized to serve. This word also distinguishes it from other major breeds of life insurance products such as *Term Insurance* or *Whole Life*.

Last, but not least, we have the word **life** which refers to the fact that an IUL is a life insurance product.

Where does the IUL come from?

The IUL was developed in the 1990s by the insurance carriers.[4] And by **carriers**, I am referring to the life insurance companies themselves that actually develop and carry the life insurance products and are responsible for the distribution of the policy benefits (including the *death benefit*). The IUL is essentially a modern, evolved version of traditional permanent life insurance which goes back to almost a few hundred years!

So an IUL is just life insurance?

An IUL is a type of life insurance, yes, which rightfully implies the existence of a death benefit that is paid upon the death of the insured. However, an IUL may also be intentionally structured and designed to serve other financial security needs such as **saving, cash accumulation, long-term care,** and **retirement income**.

IULs can also be optimized to leverage **tax advantages** *that are unique to its asset class.*

---

[4] Al DeRemigis "Indexed Universal Life – A Crash Course slideshare.net (accessed May 24, 2021)

So, to describe an IUL as "just life insurance" would probably be overly simplistic and misleading if you tend to think of life insurance as something that simply happens when you die. On the contrary, the IUL is a relatively modern financial product so it's definitely not the kind of life insurance your grandparents got, and probably not what your parents got, either.

And by the way, it's worth mentioning that the types of life insurance I typically see being promoted on television commercials - especially the ones advertising those super low monthly rates - are typically selling a form of term life insurance. If you wanted to call any type of life insurance "just life insurance," then this would be it.

However, an IUL is so vastly different from term life insurance that even though they are both technically life insurance, you are really just comparing apples to oranges. In fact, in Chapter 7 of this book, IUL vs., you can view a direct comparison between the two and see the difference for yourself.

And as far as the IRS is concerned, it's worth knowing that Uncle Sam considers life insurance to be its own category governed by its own set of rules and tax liabilities. **The IUL, therefore, is treated differently than other traditional types of retirement accounts such as traditional IRAs and 401(k) plans.**

But where the IUL really begins to distinguish itself from the rest of the pack is when the IUL plan design is properly structured and optimized for cash accumulation and tax-free supplemental income which can be used for your retirement years (or earlier if properly funded).

And that's because not only does the IUL leverage the financial markets similarly to stock ownership and mutual funds, but it does so while retaining its life insurance identity as well -- allowing it to also benefit from the tax advantages unique to the insurance asset class.

More on that last point a little later in this chapter, but the point is that **THE IUL IS NOT JUST LIFE INSURANCE** if you have an old-fashioned conception of what life insurance is.

Like I said at the very beginning of this book, **the IUL is what I believe to be the single most powerful financial security vehicle available for Americans today.** And remember, I am saying this as someone who has been in the industry for nearly 25 years. In fact, not only is this my honest assessment given the vast array of products available across the financial landscape, but I would scream it with megaphone in hand from the mountain tops.

Keep in mind, I cannot recommend any product to you unless I get to know your financial situation and needs first. That's why the main purpose of this book is simply to educate you, the consumer, about another financial security option that you may not be aware of. The fact is I utilize various types of financial products (in addition to IULs) to help my clients facilitate their financial security needs -- from term life insurance to simple 401(k)s to annuities, as well.

That said, let me go ahead and get into the nitty gritty of why I think the IUL is such a robust product and **a worthy consideration as a potential cornerstone for one's financial security.** And to do that, I'm going to list my top twelve reasons why right now.

1. Indexed Cash Accumulation

Indexed Cash Accumulation refers to how cash value accumulates within an IUL -- which is based upon positive financial market activity -- i.e., market growth.

In other words, as long as the economy grows as indicated by the market index (or indices) associated with your IUL, then the cash value within your IUL will generally grow in similar patterns.

Remember, the "I" in "IUL" stands for "indexed," but to be more descriptive you could say that the "I" stands for *indexed cash accumulation strategy* which refers to the way in which IULs can grow (or accumulate) money.

In fact, there are three investment principles or sub-strategies that are implicitly applied with an indexed growth strategy such as an IUL -- and it's worth mentioning them to better appreciate how the IUL effectively leverages all three.

Sub-Strategy / Investment Principle #1

GROW MONEY BY LEVERAGING EARNED INTEREST

There used to be just two basic things you could do with your money. You could either a) hide it somewhere in or around your house or property or b) you could put it in a bank. The main benefit, of course, to placing your money in the bank is that your money is generally considered safer than if you had kept all your money at home and, therefore, exposed to various kinds of risks such as robbery or fire or any number of potential unfortunate events that could possibly cause you to lose your life savings in an instant.

Sure, the bank could get robbed too, but any losses in such an event would be insured by the FDIC (at least up to $250,000).

But as we all know, banks have become more than just places to keep our money safe; they have become institutions that many people use to manage, borrow, receive, and spend money as well (via checks, bank cards, and wire transfers). You can also choose to grow your money with time via interest-bearing savings accounts.

It's this principle of interest, however, that you must consider as fundamental to winning the financial game of life. In other words, you cannot be content with merely holding or possessing your money, but rather, you should strive to grow your money via the principle of interest.

The key factor is <u>TIME</u> and it can either work against you as in the case of credit card interest charges on unpaid balances you carry month to month OR it can work for you as in the form of **earned interest** which is credited or applied to your cash value accounts (such as an IUL) which naturally increases your cash value amount (or principal).

At the very least, to grow your money with time neutralizes the negative financial effects of inflation which de-values money with time. A soda at the vending machine used to cost a nickel ($0.05), but now they cost two to three dollars – in large part due to inflation. This is why it is so critical to not let your money simply slumber away in some non-interest-bearing account. Time will either hurt or help the value of your money so choose the latter.

Sub-Strategy / Investment Principle #2

GROW MONEY BY LEVERAGING FINANCIAL MARKETS

Unfortunately, the interest (cash accumulation) that is typically earned from savings accounts offered by banks are low - often times yielding under 1% to 2% per year. This low percentage of cash accumulation is why most investors who seriously want to grow their money tend to turn to other means of doing so.

This is where the stock markets come into play as they have become the arena for investors all over the world to grow their money. This is true for the simple reason that funds invested in the financial markets tend to grow higher and at a faster clip than other traditional investments such as bonds and CDs, for example, which tend to earn in the neighborhood of 5% and less than 1%, respectively. [5] [6]

The fact is that many of the world's richest, smartest, and most entrepreneurial successful people in the world invest in funds where the cash growth is based on the growth of the stock markets – and that should mean something to you. Because despite the volatility of the markets and the risk of losses assumed by the participants or the fact that one tweet could send the markets into a frenzy, many of the world's wisest investors still consider their investments in the financial markets as their best bets for growing their money the most and the fastest.

Sub-Strategy / Investment Principle #3

GROW MONEY BY LEVERAGING THE ENTIRE INDEX

You've probably heard the saying, **"a rising tide lifts all**

---

[5] Bankrate "What are today's CD rates?" Bankrate.com (accessed May 24, 2021)
[6] CNN Money "How do bond returns compare with stock returns?" money.cnn.com (accessed May 24, 2021)

boats." It's a phrase that essentially implies that if the economy is doing well (*the rising tide*), then all the participants within it will do well also (*the boats*).

This saying is also an appropriate metaphor to describe the indexed cash accumulation method that IULs utilize to credit the cash values within it. You see, what's important to remember is that not only is an IUL's cash growth linked to a financial market (or multiple markets if structured that way), *it's linked to the performance of the entire index* (*i.e., the tide*).

As an example, if you had an IUL linked to the *S&P 500*, that would ultimately mean that your cash value gains would be dependent upon the growth of the market as a whole. In other words, if the index value of a particular financial market increases, that increase signifies market growth. It's as simple as that.

Compare that to the more traditional investment strategy (and pressure) of trying to pick the winning stocks for both short-term and long-term gains. In other words, these **investment firms** are actively managing the stock portfolios within mutual funds in an effort to **beat the market** – as they pick this stock (boat) over here and that stock (boat) over there. This is the method of approach for cash accumulation for many retirement accounts dependent upon actively managed funds associated with many IRAs, 401(k)s, and government employee retirement accounts.

Here's the problem, though. That's an entirely different game that requires a bunch of specialized intelligence, software, skill, and knowledge to have a chance at success. Even with highly intelligent personnel with their ears to the floor, these firms can't always predict what's going to happen with the market such as when a company is about to tank or when one is about to take off - **which is why many of these firms not only fail to beat the market, but they fail to keep pace with the market.**

In fact, according to the famous Tony Robbins who wrote a lengthy 600+ page book on money based on interviews with some of the great economists and investors around the world, "**96% will fail to match or beat the market over any extended period.**" [7]

You see, when your cash growth is dependent upon the performance of the entire index as a whole, you are getting all the winners and the losers in your basket. Therefore, as long as there is more winning than losing, the market will grow which means the index number will increase which means your cash values within your IUL will generally increase as well.

I say "generally," by the way, because ultimately the cash value growth within an IUL will depend upon how the IUL plan design was structured in the first place. That said, the general idea is that if the market linked to an IUL is growing (as indicated by an increase of the market's index value), then so will your IUL cash value grow as well in similar proportion.

The index value of a market sort of acts as a barometer for the economy (or sectors of the economy) based upon the representation and membership of all the companies within it. For example, the S&P 500 is a stock exchange composed of 500 companies.

Here's what you need to appreciate about the whole

[7] Jacob Bergdahl "An AI tried to beat the stock market index. It failed." Medium.com (accessed May 24, 2021)

"indexing" thing though. The index investment strategy itself began as a revolutionary concept introduced and popularized by a gentleman named John Bogle, [8] considered by many to be a legend today. Again, he changed the game with one simple strategy - index investing. He created mutual funds that tracked the broader market. He promoted the concept of betting on the whole market rather than worrying about the players which are constantly changing within it. In other words, if you simply bet on the tide rising, you don't have to worry about picking the right stocks. ***As long as the economy pushes forward, so will your money.***

Fast forward to today and now index investing is a popular strategy for investors all over the world.

In fact, in 2008, Warren Buffet challenged the hedge fund industry and said that including fees, costs and expenses, **an S&P 500 index fund would outperform a hand-picked portfolio of hedge funds over 10 years**. He literally made a public million dollar bet with a hedge fund group and he won that bet. [9]

As you can see, the IUL isn't just growing money using some random method called "indexing," but rather, the ***IUL is utilizing one of the most revered, revolutionary, and proven investment strategies ever created to leverage the stock markets to grow your money.***

This is why I sometimes say that having an IUL in a way empowers you to ***invest like a pro*** by utilizing what is considered to be one of the smartest and soundest ways to leverage the financial markets for personal gain.

---

[8] Investopedia "Who is John Bogle" Investopedia.com (accessed May 24, 2021)
[9] Investopedia "Buffett's Bet with the Hedge Funds: And the Winner Is ..." Investopedia.com (accessed May 24, 2021)

2. Protection of Principal

My 2nd top reason why I consider the IUL to be an attractive consideration to serve a major role on behalf of your financial security is that **an IUL protects your principal.**

"Principal" can refer to different things in the financial world. For example, "principal" can refer to the amount of money you get from a bank loan. It can also refer to the original amount of money you deposit into an investment. When referring to an IUL, **the "principal" is considered to be the cash value recognized within the cash account of the IUL.**

But here's the great part. Even though the cash value within an IUL can increase due to market gains, it won't decrease due to market losses! In other words, you get to benefit from the upside while being protected from the downside at the same time.

That's important because as the cash value within your IUL grows in size, the more you will view it as a true nest egg of financial security. And how nice is it to know that your nest egg is protected? Very nice I imagine. And that's because not only is your IUL principal protected against the negative years, but it's also protected against market crashes or severe downswings.

So what happens if the market does have a bad year?

Good question. Well, first of all, let's clarify what a "bad year" means.

I'm assuming any year where the index value of the financial market linked to an IUL is lower than where it started at the beginning of the year to be technically *"bad"* -- so in other words, *any negative* year is a bad year.

Therefore, if the market linked to your IUL account indeed had a negative year -- well, in that case, a "0" would be entered in the credited earnings column on your IUL annual report. In other words, **the floor is set at zero** which means negative values (market losses) won't register and reduce your principal.

Compare that with someone who had traditional investments featuring securities or a stock portfolio within their IRA and 401(k) accounts. And let's pretend the market just finished the year and tanked 22%. Chances are that both the 401(k) and IRA lost a lot of money as well – maybe they're lucky and the losses are less than 22% or perhaps even scarier, maybe the losses are even greater than 22%. Ouch.

Hopefully, the market will bounce right back as it sometimes does, but sometimes the rebound may take years -- and stock market history proves that fact.

On the other hand, the principal within an IUL which could potentially represent the sum of all your hard-earned money, life savings, and sound investments is protected from those bad years.

And yet, even though you are protected against the downside and market losses with an IUL, you aren't committed to some fixed, low-interest yielding CD or savings account, either. On the contrary, **you can capture a major portion of the upside if not all of it** depending upon how your IUL is structured and what the markets gains were (I detail this further with sample scenarios in chapter 6).

But beyond all that, it's hard to put a value on the peace of mind that comes with knowing that **you can only enjoy the ups while remaining immune to the downs**. Some would say that feeling is priceless, and I would tend to agree with them.

3. The Annual Reset Provision

The 3rd reason why I consider the IUL a potentially powerful investment strategy and instrument for financial security, and planning in particular, is the wonderful feature called the **annual reset provision**.

The annual reset provision is a particular feature of IULs that truly makes it a dependable cash growing machine -- and, thankfully, it is fairly easy to understand.

In short, the annual reset provision refers to the contractual guarantee stipulated within an IUL contract which generally says that for every year there is interest credited to your principal, those gains get **locked-in!** That means **those gains are added to your principal permanently** which results in your principal getting *reset* at the new higher amount. Fantastic!

In other words, you could see it this way:

MY PRINCIPAL AMOUNT AT THE BEGINNING OF THE YEAR + CREDITED GAINS FROM THIS YEAR (if any) = MY NEW PRINCIPAL AMOUNT FOR NEXT YEAR.

For this reason, the annual reset provision is sometimes compared to a ratchet which is a tool which can only move in one direction until it locks into place in the next position.

And remember, as we just discussed, this new principal amount is not only able to grow the following year (if the market experiences another positive year and your IUL is structured to capture the gains), but it is protected from any market losses as well. In other words, **no matter what happens "next" year, this year's credited gains are forever added to your cash account within your IUL.**

You see, whatever amount of **interest** or **credit** or **cash accumulation** (insurance companies use all three terms to refer to the cash value growth) your cash account within your IUL officially receives will typically be determined on **an annual basis** -- usually on the anniversary of your IUL official start date.

For example, if you setup your IUL on March 6th and the market index linked to your account was exclusively configured to be the *S&P 500*, then every year on March 6th your IUL's net gain (if any) will essentially be determined by the index value on that date and compared to the index value that was registered the preceding year. For any years that result in net losses -- which would imply an economic recession of some degree -- obviously, there will be no gain to capture in those years since that would mean that the market index value decreased. However, at least your principal you started with at the beginning of the year stays intact and won't decrease at all due to the market downturn -- no matter how bad it is.

Compare that with traditional retirement accounts which do not possess such a provision. For example, you may have one, two, three, let's say four good years in a row of positive growth -- and then in the fifth year, potentially suffer a 30% loss. But here's the kicker -- that 30% loss affects your entire cash accumulated for the lifetime of your account up to that point -- which in this case would include **ALL of the gains you made from the previous four years,** not just the fifth year. Ouch.

The truth is that the stock markets are a lot like the weather. You may tend to have decent weather most of the time, but then out of nowhere a huge storm wreaks utter havoc and destruction - causing damage to something that may have taken you years to build.

And, unfortunately, all it takes is one corrupt CEO or one bogus comment on social media or another global pandemic or bad politics to send the markets tumbling.

That's why I sometimes think of traditional retirement plans which are heavily invested in stock-filled mutual funds as being **ALL-IN** on every hand in the game of poker. All it takes is one bad hand or one bad year to mess things up and sabotage many positive years. Just ask the folks who experienced the stock market crash of 1929. Depending upon who you ask and what numbers you are looking at, it took 10-25 years to fully recover.

Sure, the market has been great for long-term investors (which is why I want to leverage it, remember), but the swings along the way may still potentially be financially devastating for many people. To me, that's not financial security. **You cannot win the financial game of life by having a considerable portion of your life's savings exposed to uncapped losses every single day all the time.** That's potentially exposing your nest egg of life savings money to the risk of significant losses every single day and every single year for the lifetime of the retirement account! And given today's world which seems crazier and more unpredictable than ever before, to me, that's an opportunity to lose the game every day. No thank you.

The point is that in case there is a very bad economic year, your IUL principal won't suffer the same blow to principal as many traditional retirement accounts would otherwise experience. In fact, assuming positive years existed, as you view your IUL annual reports after several years of investment, **the graph of your cash accumulation will begin to look like a staircase.** And that is because your IUL principal (cash value amount) will only go **sideways and up, but never down**. This is the result when you combine protection of principal with the annual reset provision.

On the other hand, for those who are fully vested in the stock market -- like those who have traditional IRAs, 401(k)s, and other stock-heavy mutual fund portfolios --

they will have their cash accumulation graph looking more like a heart-rate monitor with a bunch of ups and downs.

4. Tax-Free Death Benefit

I could easily have placed this IUL benefit at the top of my list because it refers to the essence of what a life insurance product is all about -- which is the monetary death benefit which serves as a financial life saver.

As I told you in chapter 4, the death benefit refers to the monetary lump sum payment that the life insurance company pays to the beneficiaries when the insured person dies. In other words, when an insured person dies, specific people will receive a check, tax-free.

Practically speaking, the death benefit usually serves as financial protection of some sort to help mitigate the financial burdens that arise when the insured dies as well as to compensate for the future loss income that the insured would have earned had the insured stayed alive. This is assuming the insured person has family members which depend on his/her income for financial stability, a.k.a. "dependents."

Whether the death benefit is meant to serve as mortgage insurance, lifestyle insurance, or make-sure-my-family-has-food-on-the-table insurance, the point is that *life insurance is one of the most important and powerful financial products that money can buy.*

Just ponder for a minute that *magical moment* when you have acquired an IUL or life insurance policy of some kind. And let's pretend that you started that policy plan with a couple hundred dollars – say $200. There will be more premiums to pay, of course, but I'm just talking about right now in terms of what it takes to get started.

The magic is that you invested $200, but by doing so, you are possibly entitled to a pot of money that is 6-figures large. Ultimately, your age will be the deciding factor in terms of determining the possible death benefit amount based on the premium schedule you commit to, but the leverage that is secured the moment your policy contract is approved is almost magical.

Less magical is the moment someone first invests into a traditional IRA or 401(k) plan. For example, let's say soon after that someone invests $200 into a new 401(k) plan, that person dies. That $200 in the 401(k) is still just $200. Actually, to be technical, it's probably worth a little less than $200 due to taxes which will have to be paid upon withdrawal. But the point is there is no magical leverage there. Essentially what was put in is what will get out.

But that's not the case with life insurance because what you get out may be MUCH MORE than what you put in.

Another point regarding the death benefit from life insurance is that **it's given to the beneficiaries tax-free.** That's clearly significant because if your policy face value is $1,000,000 dollars, your beneficiaries will receive one million dollars -- not $800,000 or $700,000 or $500,000 due to taxes, but rather, all one million of it.

Compare that to what happens to your traditional investments when bequeathed due to your passing. Unless it's a ROTH, chances are whatever amount that is ultimately given to your beneficiaries will be significantly less than whatever the balance was at the time of death -- and the main culprit will be taxes that had to be paid up before distribution.

There's one more point I want to make here and it's this: while I may be literally speaking about a tax-free death benefit, at the heart of the matter I'm really talking about leaving a legacy.

Technically speaking, legacy can refer to the money you leave for your beneficiaries, but generally speaking, **"legacy" refers to what you leave behind.**

Whether that IUL tax-free death benefit you leave for your beneficiaries and family is meant to enable your dependents to survive financially without you or whether it's meant to serve as the ultimate gift to empower them to pursue their dreams and live a comfortable life -- either way, that becomes your legacy.

Rest in Peace. We've all heard of this phrase before and my very simply question for you is can you truly rest in peace if you leave behind a chaotic mess of debts for your loved ones? Can you rest in peace if you fail to leave any financial support behind which may indirectly force your family to move out of the house? Can you rest in peace by not knowing if your children will be able to afford college education or a down payment on their first house?

I ask you these questions not to give you a guilt trip, but rather, to simply get you thinking about some important matters especially if you already have a family or dependents. Again, we're talking about your legacy here.

And even for those of you who may not have a family yet or don't plan to -- even then, you may still want to leave a legacy behind. Who am I to say you may not have a legacy need? You may have a non-profit mission you want to sustain. You may have a museum or church or other institution you want to leave the ultimate gift for. Again, for those who value the concept, we're talking about your legacy here.

5. Tax-Free Living Benefits

Let me ask you a question.

Do you think there is any chance you may become significantly sick or critically hurt by accident in the future? Especially as you grow older?

If your answer is "yes," (and even as a person in perfect health right now you may have wisely answered 'yes'), then you will be interested in what I'm about to tell you.

And it's this: another benefit to having an IUL is that many of them typically include (at least as an option) something called *living benefits.*

These living benefits take the form of financial support that you don't have to die to benefit from. That's why they are called "living" benefits. And, basically, how it works is that your insurance company will allow you to tap into the *death benefit money of your IUL while you are alive* if specific (unfortunate) health conditions arise such as critical, chronic, or terminal illness.

Think about it. As an example, if someone had an IUL with a $500,000 death benefit and that person was to suffer a bad car accident which resulted in him/her being in critical condition, health insurance may not cover all the healthcare costs, physical therapy, or other indirect costs associated with the accident. On top of that, even if your health insurance covered most of the costs, the accident would probably result in a loss of income, too. Well, in this case, this person would be able to tap into that $500,000 death benefit and use that money as needed, tax-free. What a life saver!

Keep in mind, every insurance company and IUL will define these living benefits slightly differently so it's important to know the details and consult with your IUL agent. In fact, not every IUL will include such provisions. That said, if you want living benefits simply make sure your IUL agent provides you a policy plan that includes it.

But again, think about it. With the right IUL, you could potentially protect yourself against what would otherwise potentially be a bankrupting situation.

With the extra financial support of your living benefits, you would also probably be able to ensure you get the quality healthcare you truly desire when you need it most.

And we're not just talking about rare, unheard-of health conditions here. We're talking about illnesses and conditions that could result from the likes of heart attacks, stroke, Alzheimer's, dementia, and other conditions.

The IUL policy contract will define exactly how one may qualify for living benefits. That said, generally speaking, certain health conditions, once diagnosed by a medical doctor, will immediately trigger access to living benefits. Other health conditions could potentially qualify someone for living benefits as well if he/she is unable to perform 2 out of the 6 **Activities of Daily Living (ADLs).** These ADLs are universally recognized within the life insurance industry.

They are:

a) Bathing
b) Dressing
c) Eating
d) Transferring
e) Toileting
f) Continence

Living benefits are an important financial security consideration in my opinion because even if you are in perfect health right now, how can you truly say to yourself that there's no chance something could happen to you in the future? Of course you can't.

Another thing to keep in mind is that if you did have an IUL with living benefits and qualified to use them because of a critical, chronic, or terminal illness as defined in your IUL contract, then whatever amount of money you end up using would simply be subtracted from your death benefit.

So, using our previous example, if the person who suffered from the car accident ended up using $100,000 to ensure the best quality care and replace his/her lost income, then their $500,000 original death benefit amount would reduce to $400,000.

But consider what happened in my example scenario here. This person was able to tap into $100,000 of extra financial support while alive from the death benefit!

At the end of the day, living benefits translates to potential extra financial support in your neediest of times -- which could end up being a real life saver.

6. Potential Tax-Free Income

There is another feature of most IULs that truly makes it special and it's this: with an IUL you have the possibility of generating **a tax-free supplemental income stream that may last many years if not, practically speaking, for a lifetime!**

Basically, the way it works is that once your cash account within your IUL reaches a specific threshold amount (based on your premium contributions and indexed cash accumulation), a stream of supplemental tax-free annual income will become available to you.

How soon you can qualify for this income stream will primarily depend on how aggressively you decide to fund your IUL via your premium payment schedule, your age when you started, and the indexed cash accumulation your account earns over time.

Once available, that income stream can be configured to begin when you want and last however long you wish in terms of number of years.

There are some key considerations to keep in mind here.

First of all, the amount of supplemental income available to you will, in part, be determined by the number of years you configure it to last. In other words, if you choose to set your supplemental annual income to last 25 years (from age 65 to 90 years old), that income amount will be higher than the income amount generated if you had configured it to last 10 years longer (35 years long) until the age of 100.

It's worth emphasizing one of the greatest attractions of

this plan design which is that this annual supplemental income stream is distributed to you TAX-FREE via the policy loan feature.

Compare that with traditional qualified accounts which must be taxed upon distribution. Whatever number you see in your account is not what you will get. What you receive will be a number that is smaller than what you see and you won't know what that final net income amount of money is until you, your accountant, or tax professional does the work.

Anytime you can muster up tax-free income, I call that a winning move and financial strategy that will truly empower you with the best chance to win the financial game of life.

7. Tax Advantages

You may have noticed a theme here so far and that's the theme of TAX-FREE.

Already on my Top 12 Reasons List I've mentioned the following tax advantages to you:

a) TAX-FREE Death Benefit
b) TAX-FREE Living Benefits
c) Potential TAX-FREE Income

And yet there's more tax advantages I haven't mentioned to you yet. In fact, if I was to continue my mini-list of major IUL tax advantages for you, I would add these two:

d) TAX-FREE GROWTH
e) TAX-FREE ACCESSIBILITY

TAX-FREE GROWTH

Cash accumulates within an IUL on a tax-deferred basis. **This means that the cash account within an IUL grows tax-free.**

Normally, a retirement account that is growing tax-deferred (like a traditional 401(k) or IRA plan) generally implies that the taxes which would normally have to be paid every year on the earnings are instead delayed or "pushed" into the future and are paid when you pull out the money or upon distribution.

Tax deferral is generally considered to be a tax advantage because the idea is that:

a) you get to pay fewer taxes in the now (in the current year) since your contributions to such plans are usually tax-deductible

b) Your money in a tax-deferred account is allowed to grow tax-free until the money is withdrawn in the future

c) There is a chance that when you retire you will be in a lower tax-bracket because you will be making less income -- and therefore pay a lower rate of taxes when you begin to receive money from your tax-deferred accounts

So again, technically speaking, the cash accumulated earnings within an IUL is tax-deferred which means it grows tax-free.

But what follows next is where things begin to get really interesting…

TAX-FREE ACCESS

Unlike traditional tax-deferred accounts which must be taxed upon withdrawal or distribution, **the cash within an IUL may be essentially accessed tax-free.**

You see, while technically speaking, IULs grow tax-deferred, practically speaking, one can legally avoid the deferred taxes by utilizing a **policy loan feature** unique to IULs. By utilizing this policy loan feature, you need not pay taxes on your IUL cash accumulation because technically you didn't withdraw the money from your IUL.

I am not a tax professional and you should always consult with your accountant or tax professional when dealing with your tax affairs. It is also important to recognize that the policy loan feature I speak of must be applied properly with the assumption that the IUL was structured properly as well to begin with. Your agent and insurance carrier will assist you with this as necessary. Lastly, there are circumstances which could trigger a taxable event (of the deferred taxes) when seeking to distribute money from an IUL (such as a pure withdrawal above a certain amount or your policy lapsing) so it's important to do so with the aid of your licensed agent or insurance company to ensure you do so properly.

That all said, the practical net effect of taking advantage of the policy loan feature within IULs is tax-free access to an amount of money equal to whatever cash value amount is actually recognized within the IUL cash account. The practical implication of this is worth repeating. **An IUL essentially allows your money to grow tax-free while allowing tax-free access as well.**

I know that the word "loan" may scare some of you a bit, but don't let it. For starters, this policy loan feature works does not act like your typical loan where you have to apply to receive it or it shows up on your credit report. On the contrary, it's a rather genius application that the insurance companies came up with when they created the IUL in the first place. In fact, utilizing the policy loan feature is a rather routine and systematic procedure since that is the typical way people access their IUL cash values -- and it's at the heart of what makes the IUL a truly unique asset.

It's worth mentioning that the tax-deferred characteristic of 401(k)s and other similarly structured mutual fund investments is actually promoted as a selling point - and for good reason. You see, since the money in those accounts are growing tax-deferred, your money is not deflated by taxes every year - which in effect allows a bigger pot of money to benefit from compound interest.

The only problem is that once you've grown your nest egg to its biggest size given your diligent savings, Uncle Sam swoops in at the end of the day to get his share. However, instead of taxing you years ago on a smaller amount of money, he now gets to tax the big pot of savings you have accrued over decades of time.

It's debatable over the long run which is better - to pay taxes now or later. There are mathematicians and financial analysts on both sides of that argument. For me, I simply prefer to know that the number I'm looking at year to year is a tax-free number which makes my retirement planning much easier to figure out. Plus, I simply love the fact that Uncle Sam will not tax my nest egg when its reached maturity. In short, I rather pay taxes now and simply use that money to setup my tax-free growing IUL, but to be clear, that's just my personal preference.

In practical terms, what does this mean?

Well, let's say for example you are setting aside a portion of every paycheck you get from your employer and investing in a 401(k). Let's pretend your pre-tax paycheck amount is $3,600 and you have chosen to invest $200 into a 401(k). Because 401(k)s grow tax-deferred, rather than, being taxed based on $3,600, the $200 for your 401(k) is taken out first, which means your taxable income becomes $3,400 (not $3,600). This means you will pay less tax on each paycheck. However, that pre-tax (not taxed yet) $200 now has a tax liability. Therefore, whatever amount of money that $200 grows to be will eventually be taxed based on the number it grew to.

Conversely, let's pretend that instead of investing into a 401(k), you decide to invest into your IUL instead. As a consequence, you don't get any special pre-tax treatment like you do with the 401(k) which means that you will pay taxes on your full $3600 paycheck. Whatever money is leftover after taxes is your "after-tax" money. From that money, you decide to invest $200 into your IUL. The great news from here on out is that the $200 will grow tax-free, but whatever amount it accrues to will eventually be accessible tax-free via the policy loan feature of IULs.

At the end of the day, it's up to and your tax advisors to decide what you do from a tax point-of-view, but as you can see, understanding the tax liabilities that come with particular investments is important.

8. Plan Versatility

Dictionary.com defines **versatility** as "the state or quality of being useful for or easily adapted to various tasks, styles, fields of endeavor, purposes, etc."

This is the perfect word to describe the IUL because it is truly a versatile financial vehicle. The IUL can be flexed, stretched, applied and adapted to various financial purposes to meet one's specific financial needs and desires – which, of course, makes me happy because I am able to customize an IUL to my client.

In fact, to remind you, the "U" in IUL refers to "Universal" which is essentially a nod to the versatility of an IUL.

An IUL can be optimized for wealth preservation, tax-advantages, or retirement income. It can be used as a savings vehicle for the near future (such as a college education fund) or for supplemental retirement income. The applications are many and varied.

One of the main reasons why IULs are as customizable as they are is due to the existence of particular **provisions** and **riders** that are commonly considered as options or included when establishing an IUL.

These provisions and riders are essentially clauses that define specific features of a life insurance or IUL policy contract. Some of these provisions or riders will alter or adjust a policy feature or benefit in some way. Some of these provisions, and in particular, riders, offer additional features and benefits that may address other possible life scenarios for which the rider may more suitably meet the client's needs in that situation.

Finally, the IUL product, itself, may be leveraged, as well. For example, and IUL may be leveraged to secure a 3rd party loan as collateral. An IUL may also serve as its own bank and serve as the source for funds as a loan.

The IUL may also be integrated with other financial products, too. In fact, sometimes when setting up multiple financial products for my clients at the same time, I am using funds from one account to systematically fund another.

As a prime example of the IUL's versatility, I encourage you to read the bonus chapter at the end of this book called "The 5-Year Retirement Plan" which will discuss how an IUL's benefits may be amplified even more than usual.

9. Simplicity & Scope of One

One of my favorite overall characteristics of the IUL is its capacity to provide a wide scope of benefits with the simplicity of one plan or account. This is why I truly consider the IUL a worthy candidate to potentially serve as a fundamental or central role in one's overall financial security plan.

With a single IUL account, one may grow their money using the financial markets like the big boys.

With a single account one may protect their principle against the downside and, yet, still capture the upside.

With a single account, I can position my money in a tax-deferred status, allowing earnings to grow tax-free, while eventually accessing those cash values tax-free.

With a single account I can position my money in such a way so as to possibly generate a tax-free supplemental income stream that may last for decades!

With a single account, I can protect my family, my causes,

and my legacy with a monetary death benefit.

With a single account I can protect myself from the sudden financial stress that could arise out of suddenly not being able to pay the bills due to some critical, chronic, or critical health condition that could arise from a multitude of possible unfortunate and unpredictable events or medical downturns of life.

As you can see, the IUL is clearly a robust, multi-purpose financial plan and product that truly makes it a worthy champion for your financial security.

That all said, you should also know that people who get IULs often get multiple IULs - for each child, your spouse, nephews and nieces, etc. In fact, for a family I do exactly that and will often setup multiple IULs at the same time.

10. Scalability

Next on my list of reasons why I consider the IUL a worthy financial product is its scalability.

And by "scalability," I am referring to an IUL's capability to change in size. And by "size," I am actually referring to the following:

CAN BE STARTED WITH A LITTLE MONEY

For starters, **an IUL can be started with little money** -- meaning you can setup an IUL with a low monthly premium rate as low as about $30 a month or a dollar a day for young people or for a $100 a month for older adults. This makes an IUL very affordable to most Americans.

Ideally, a good rule of thumb in terms of how much to invest, save, or contribute into a retirement/savings account is to do at least $200 a month while in your 20s, $300 a month while in your 30s, $400 while in your 40s, and $500 while in your 50s.

Also, it's important to note that, naturally, your age will affect the cost of insurance which, in turn, will affect minimum premium amounts to target specific financial goals. Some people will get started funding their IUL on the smaller side (in terms of death benefit or premiums) because they have the mindset that they will gradually increase coverage or investment with time as one's budget allows.

CAN BE STARTED WITH A LOT OF MONEY

Just as an IUL can be started with a little money and a low monthly premium rate so can **an IUL be started with a lot of money.**

By "a lot of money" I mean someone could commit to a very high monthly premium schedule in excess of $1000 per month for years on end OR **someone could literally front-load an IUL with a large sum of money over a few years if desired.**

When you consider for a moment the contribution limits that currently exist for traditional retirement accounts, you will find that you can put much more money into an IUL.

Now keep in mind, in order to contribute a large sum of money, that would require the IUL to be structured with a death benefit that is typically large as well. The larger death benefit amount allows for a larger cash value to continue to grow tax-free. If you stuff too much money into an IUL too soon, it could transform into a modified endowment which will have the consequence of turning your cash accumulation into taxable income. The good news is that your insurance company will typically adjust these policies for you so that you stay in the tax-free zone, so to speak.

That said, with larger death benefits, comes larger IUL cash values, larger legacies, larger living benefits, and probably much larger tax-free income streams, as well.

11. Churches & Non-Profits

Shifting things a little bit, number 11 on my list applies to organizations – specifically, non-profits and churches.

Life insurance, in general, may be particularly suited for churches and other non-profit organizations which are mission-based due to the legacy component which provides for a monetary death benefit.

The easiest application, of course, would be for the Pastor or head minister to secure a policy and then assign the church as the beneficiary (in addition to his/her family if need be). In this case, the church, itself, may choose to acquire and fund the policy.

Making the church or non-profit organization the beneficiaries of the policy, of course, creates wealth for the organization which can be used to sustain its programs and missions. Whether the IUL is funded by the pastor or the church, it doesn't effectively matter.

That said, a church or non-profit organization could also choose to structure an IUL so that it may eventually generate supplemental income for a long-time executive leader, pastor, or head minister as a gesture of gratitude and reward in exchange for decades of dedicated service (like a pension plan) -- which could be leveraged as an incentive if desired.

Finally, churches and successful non-profit organizations are always seeking to expand. They want to grow the congregation or outreach, buy more land, hire more people, etc. Therefore, securing a loan will often be a solution to do so and here's where an IUL or life insurance policy can potentially assist because it can be effectively used as collateral to secure large loans if you have a large policy to back it up. I've been privy to many situations where a bank loan was able to be secured due to the effective leveraged use of a life insurance policy or IUL.

12. Businesses & Corporations

Last, but not least, just as churches and non-profits can utilize an IUL so can businesses and corporations, as well.

Whether the business is owned or managed by several partners or by one person, an IUL can be setup to leave a legacy for the business so that it may survive without you.

In the case of a multiple executives, managers, or owners, an IUL can also be leveraged as an incentive for years of dedicated service whereby the business buys the IUL for the key employee or executive (like keyman insurance).

Multiple beneficiaries are possible so one could effectively leave a legacy for their business and family with one policy.

When used as a work incentive, an IUL can serve as a powerful recruitment tool to get and retain the best talent.

IULs purchased for key personnel can also serve to help them in case they get sick in a way that allows them to tap into the living benefits.

There are also some potential tax write-offs that are potentially possible when buying policies for your employees.

Finally, what about all the employees of the company, in general?

Well, sadly, most employers still don't offer an IUL as part of their benefits packages or retirement savings options, but that is simply because they (CEOs, CFOs and HR personnel in particular) are still unaware or haven't been offered it yet. Meanwhile the 401(k) has sort of become the de facto retirement account for America these days.

But the good news is that the tide is changing as more corporate executives, business owners, and HR personnel get educated on IULs.

Think about it. If you are a business owner with employees, then at the very least, you could offer the option of an IUL in the form of an automatic paycheck deduction. By doing so, you could promote the fact that you offer a benefits plan option that provides the many features of the IUL, making employment at your business that much more attractive.

For the business owners or HR folks that are truly seeking to attain and retain the best talent, adding an IUL-based retirement/savings plan is a great way to distinguish you amongst your competitors. By adding an IUL-based plan to your current benefits package, you would be creating a truly robust benefits package that's difficult to rival. In fact, some business owners are choosing IUL-based plans in leu of traditional retirement plans such as a 401(k).

6

TOO GOOD TO BE TRUE?

When people first discover the IUL and begin to really digest all of the bona fide and potential benefits and features that this financial product is capable of offering, a **common reaction I often see is one of shock and awe.**

Soon after that, however, many people will begin to question or doubt the IUL's legitimacy. And I get it. I totally get it -- because once you've lived a little, it's true that most things that sound too good to be true are, in fact, not true.

Not only is this skepticism normal, I would argue that it's good and prudent – especially when it comes to financial instruments that you are considering for yourself or your family.

That's why I don't take it personal when people get testy, defensive, or simply refuse to accept what I'm telling them sometimes with regards to the IUL.

Afterall, how could something this good be something you haven't heard of before, right?

How come you've never had your employer offer it to you as a savings option or as one of those automatic paycheck deduction options like your 401(k) plan?

Why hasn't your financial advisor (if you have one) or your accountant mentioned it to you before, either?

These are all great questions -- and I promise to answer each one of them in this chapter as well as some other FAQ I often hear.

But for starters, let me just say this: the IUL is the real deal. It's not a myth. It's not make-believe. It's not fantasy or science-fiction or something from the future. It's as legitimate as your driver's license and I've been helping people attain this asset which is available in all 50 states for years.

That all said, there are some legitimate questions about the IUL worth answering which will hopefully offer you some further insight and understanding.

What's the catch?

What's the catch? Usually, we ask this question to dig for that one detail or stipulation or condition that is unagreeable, right? Well, in that case, I don't think there is a "catch" with regards to the IUL as long as you are properly educated on what it is, how it works, and have a need for the financial benefits it provides.

That said, I do think it's good to recognize some general key facts and potential limitations regarding the IUL when considering it.

Not Really A Catch #1
You recognize that the IUL is a life insurance product.

As I explained to you in chapters 4 and 5, an IUL is a life insurance product. And while the IUL has a cash value component and cash accumulation component and a potential for supplemental income, obviously another core component is the pure life insurance part which is the monetary death benefit.

This means that you should have a life insurance need of some sort (refer to chapter 4 for reasons why people get life insurance) as you consider an IUL. If you do have a need for life insurance, then an IUL is a strategic and sound way to acquire life insurance while also purposefully pursuing financial security for the future utilizing sound investment strategies and leveraging the financial markets.

Not Really A Catch #2
You recognize that there is a cost of insurance.

Naturally, because an IUL provides a death benefit (and possibly other benefits based on riders, etc.) there is a **cost of insurance.** That means that when you pay your premiums, a portion of that premium is allocated to the cost of insurance. The rest of the premium as well as the surplus that results from time is essentially placed into your cash account within your IUL.

The younger you are the, the smaller the cost of insurance will be – as little as 20% of the total premium. The older you are, the more the cost of insurance will be – as much as the majority percentage of the total premium. This is why you would ideally begin an IUL while you are relatively young. That said, for older adults, you may still reach target face values and income streams, but you may have to invest more to reach those goals because you are essentially trying to catch up.

One more point I should make in this regard is you need to remember to account for taxes. Tax brackets currently range from 10-37% depending upon your income.[10] Historically, tax rates have existed beyond 60%, 70% and even 90% in times of war.[11] Those facts plus the fact that IULs provide tax-free growth plus tax-free access makes the following question seem very appropriate.

Would you rather pay a percentage of your money <u>for taxes</u> OR would you rather pay a percentage of your money <u>for a monetary death benefit (legacy), living benefits, and a potential tax-free supplemental income stream that may last, practically, for a lifetime?</u>

Not Really A Catch #3
You cannot let your policy lapse.

By policy "lapse" I essentially mean "expire" and by "expire," I mean that a policy contract becomes null and void and will no longer provide you a death benefit.

---

[10] Tax Foundation "2021 Federal Income Tax Brackets and Rates" taxfoundation.com (accessed May 24, 2021)
[11] Wikipedia "History of taxation in the United States" wikipedia.com (accessed May 24, 2021)

A life insurance policy will lapse when you stop making your premium payments. Every policy and carrier will have their own stipulations on any grace periods that may exist or how you may re-instate a policy that has lapsed.

The good news is that once you've had an IUL for a few years or so, you will begin to create enough cash value that it will essentially act as a backup in case you can't afford your premiums for a period of time for whatever reason.

COVID-19 was a great example of this. I had some clients tell me that they could no longer pay the premiums because they lost their job due to the pandemic. In many cases, what I did was simply re-structure their IUL so that they only had to pay the minimum amount or no longer had to fund it at all and use the cash value on hand to keep the policy alive. In one case, I re-structured the IUL cash value inside the policy to pay the policy for the next 5 years.

Then, whenever these people are financially ready to resume consistent premium payments, they can do so, and if need be, we can re-structure the IUL again.

Meanwhile, the IUL remains active and in good standing the entire time during the interim and that way my clients and their families remain financially protected.

Not Really A Catch #4
An IUL must be adequately funded or adequately grown in size for the tax-free supplemental income stream to be available.

As I mentioned in chapter 5, The 3-Letter Word Explained, the IUL is capable of providing tax-free income that can be structured to last 20, 25, or even 40 years or longer if you want and, therefore, practically for a lifetime. This is why this benefit is sometimes referred to as "lifetime income."

But the point is that this income stream requires your IUL cash values to reach minimum thresholds so as to allow for such income. Again, I don't really consider this a "catch," but more of a "of course it does."

I mean, think about it. If you were to start an IUL with a few hundred dollars, you are already benefitting from the tremendous immediate leverage of turning that small investment into a potential 6-fgure death benefit and source of living benefit protection, but to also qualify for an income stream in addition to that death benefit, clearly your cash values will have to reach a certain monetary point first for this benefit to be then made available.

All of this is to really say that, like most retirement accounts, ***investing into an IUL is a long-term financial security strategy.*** You could say that this is the nature of an IUL since it is a form of permanent life insurance.

I know what you're thinking now...

How will you know when this income stream will be available and how much income will you get?

The customary way to get a feel for what sized income stream you may be able to generate based on your policy and premiums is to get a personalized IUL illustration.

An IUL illustration is a hypothetical forecast report of your IUL performance over time on an annual basis.

The IUL illustration will be personalized to you and will

therefore consider your age, death benefit face value, desired premium payments and schedule, and any riders or configurable optimizations that were done to suit your financial needs and situation.

An illustration demonstrates how the various account values of significance may vary and grow over time based on hypothetical market conditions and on how your particular IUL is structured by your IUL agent -- which should be constructed to serve your communicated financial goals and needs. These reports use conservative single-digit average rates of market growth around 6 to 8%. In recent years, the reality is that my clients have been doing 3x or greater than that. That said, past performance cannot predict future results.

Because the potential tax-free supplemental annual income is often desired, many clients of mine will ask me to optimize the IUL in a way that targets a specific income range. In this way, it's similar to financial planning that works backward to know what you have to do in the now.

Not Really A Catch #5
The amount of money your IUL's cash account earns will ultimately depend upon your IUL's indexed crediting methods.
This is a key point to recognize because as I've mentioned before, not all IULs are created equal. That's because it's the insurance companies that carry IULs that ultimately determine their provisions (within the scope of the law).

The index or indexed crediting method refers to the specific formula that an IUL policy contract uses to determine how much of the market upside an IUL will capture. Variables worth mentioning which may be included (but not limited to) to the indexed crediting formula are:

a) Participation Rates
b) Margins (fees)
c) Caps

In other words, when the index which is linked to an IUL has a net-positive year in terms of percentage points, the indexed crediting method that your IUL is governed by will determine what percentage of that market growth will ultimately be algorithmically applied and added to your principal.

So, for example, let's say that the S&P 500 which was solely linked to your IUL just had a great year and grew 28% relative to your IUL. I'm using this number because the S&P actually did grow over 28% in 2019 and over 29% in 2013.[12] That said, keep in mind, it's the IUL's anniversary date that determines when a year begins and ends as far as your IUL's performance is concerned.

The question becomes how much of that 28% market upside will your IUL capture? This is where those other variables I mentioned come into play such as participation rates, margins, and caps. So, let's look at a few simplified scenarios of these variables at work for educational purposes only.

Scenario A
Market Gain at end of the year is 28%
Participation Rate is 100%
No Margin
Cap of 12%
Principal at beginning of the year was $50,000

---

[12] Macrotrends "S&P 500 Index - 90 Year Historical Chart" macrotrends.net (accessed May 24, 2021"

Caps act as maximums or ceilings on what is capturable. Therefore, in this scenario, your IUL cash account (principal) will be credited with a 12% gain. In other words, your IUL cash account grew $6,000 which, don't forget, will then be permanently added to your protected principal for the following year via the annual reset provision. So, next year your reset protected principal will be $56,000.

Scenario B
Market Gain at end of the year is 28%
Participation Rate is 100%
Margin is 4%
No Cap
Principal at beginning of the year was $50,000

Margins act as front-loaded fees that must be paid up first before tapping into the rest of the gain. Therefore, in this scenario, your IUL cash account (principal) will be credited with a whopping 24% gain. In other words, your IUL cash account grew $12,000 which, don't forget, will then be permanently added to your protected principal for the following year via the annual reset provision. So, next year your reset protected principal will be $62,000.

Scenario C
Market Gain at end of the year is 28%
Participation Rate is 120%
No Margin
Cap of 12%
Principal at beginning of the year was $50,000

Participations Rates act as another factor that may be under or over 100% which will affect the final official credited gain. Therefore, in this scenario, your IUL cash account (principal) will ultimately be credited with a gain of $7,200. Notice how this is a little higher than Scenario A which had a 100% participation rate. Again, don't forget, this gain will be permanently added to your protected principal for the following year via the annual reset provision. So, next year your reset protected principal will be $57,200.

As you can see, with the 28% market upside, the uncapped strategy was the big winner here and that's because it was able to capture over 85% of the upside.

This is why I often utilize uncapped strategies in my IULs. That said, it's worth mentioning that many IULs (and brokerages who sell IULs) do not offer uncapped IUL strategies. In fact, my competitors are usually surprised to hear that not only do I offer products with those capabilities, but that I have been doing so for years.

What if, however, the market had a relatively flat year and grew 3%. Let's quickly run through those scenarios using the rest of the same numbers.

Scenario A2
Market Gain at end of the year is 3%
Participation Rate is 100%
No Margin
Cap of 12%
Principal at beginning of the year was $50,000

In this scenario, your IUL cash account (principal) will be credited with the full 3% gain ($1,500).

Scenario B2
Market Gain at end of the year is 3%
Participation Rate is 100%
Margin is 4%

No Cap
Principal at beginning of the year was $50,000

In this scenario, your IUL cash account (principal) will not be credited with any gain because the 4% margin was not surpassed.

Scenario C2
Market Gain at end of the year is 3%
Participation Rate is 120%
No Margin
Cap of 12%
Principal at beginning of the year was $50,000

In this scenario, your IUL cash account (principal) will be credited with $1,800 and, therefore, slightly more than Scenario A2 due to the higher participation rate.

As you can see here, with the low 3% market upside, the capped strategy with the higher participation rate was the winner here as it captured 120% of the upside.

So, while the uncapped strategy was the big winner for large-gain years (in term of total cash accumulated), the capped strategies were the winners for the low-gain years (in terms of total cash accumulated).

It's worth noting I like to use both strategies, capped and uncapped, at the same time so that my clients will always earn money in positive market years, period.

Also, please keep in mind, these were just some basic scenarios to illustrate how these other key variables come into play. Ultimately, the stipulations within your IUL policy contract will determine how gains are credited and every carrier has their own nuanced algorithms for how they calculate cash value gains inside your IUL.

Finally, let's run it one more time with a mid-range percentage of market growth at 10% and see what happens.

Scenario A3
Market Gain at end of the year is 10%
Participation Rate is 100%
No Margin
Cap of 12%
Principal at beginning of the year was $50,000

In this scenario, your IUL cash account (principal) will be credited with the full 10% gain ($5,000).

Scenario B3
Market Gain at end of the year is 10%
Participation Rate is 100%
Margin is 4%
No Cap
Principal at beginning of the year was $50,000

In this scenario, your IUL cash account (principal) will capture 6% of the gain after accounting for the 4% margin which results in a net gain of $3,000.

Scenario C3
Market Gain at end of the year is 10%
Participation Rate is 120%
No Margin
Cap of 12%
Principal at beginning of the year was $50,000

In this scenario, your IUL cash account (principal) will be credited with $6,000 and, therefore, slightly more than

Scenario A3 due to the higher participation rate.

As you can see here, with the mid-range 10% market upside, once again, the capped strategies out-performed the uncapped strategies because they captured all of the upside -- with the one with the higher participation rate being the ultimate winner here. That said, the uncapped strategy still captured 60% of the upside.

In fact, if you play with the numbers in these examples, you'll notice that:

When focused on market upside performance:

- All three strategies in Scenario 1 resulted in an overall 60% capture of the high 28% market upside.

- All three strategies in Scenario 2 resulted in an overall 73% capture of the low 3% market upside.

- All three strategies in Scenario 3 resulted in an overall 93% capture of the mid-range 10% market upside.

When focused on IUL strategy:

- The capped strategy in all three scenarios resulted in an overall 61% capture of the market upside.

- The uncapped strategy in all three scenarios resulted in an overall 73% capture of the market upside.

- The capped strategy with bonus participation rate resulted in an overall 73% capture of the market.

And when focused on all scenarios and strategies:

- The average percentage of the market upside captured was 76%

- The cumulative actual percentage of the market upside captured was 69%

Also, I could run three more scenarios where the market loses money, but you already know that your principal will not lose money based on negative market performance so we don't have to do that :)

So, as you can see by these example scenarios, how your IUL is strategically structured does matter, **but the good news is that regardless of strategy employed, your IUL is positioned to grow over the long-term by grabbing a good portion of the upside while you never have to worry about the downside.**

Of all the "catches" I mention, this may be arguably the most "catching," so to speak. But let me ask you a question. If you knew that you could grab a good portion of the annual market upside every year (when existent), but you never had to worry about market losses, would that sound good to you?

If it does, you're not alone. In fact, listen to what Karen Terry, assistant managing director of insurance research at LIMRA, a leading insurance industry group, had to say: **"Indexed universal life has been growing pretty strongly over the past decade. It's been with few exceptions the hot product in the life insurance industry."** [13]

---

[13] Greg Iacurci "Indexed universal life insurance sales continue hot streak" investmentnews.com (accessed May 24, 2021)

In fact, having dealt with thousands of clients, I can tell you that most people I talk to are more than content (if not genuinely joyful) with the idea of capturing most of the upside over the long run while knowing they are essentially immune from the downside.

So, if the market was to RECEDE (as in decrease) by 28%, 3%, or 10% year to year, isn't nice to know that your IUL wouldn't lose principal due to the market downturns?

And for those who do happen to see their retirement accounts lose large percentages of money due to market downturns, how long will it take for those accounts to make up for those losses? One year, two, maybe 3 or 4?

With an IUL, not only is your principal protected year to year, but again, for the years where your cash account does materialize a gain, that gain gets locked in and your principal gets reset at the higher amount for the following year. And that is a crucial fact.

How is this legal?

Like I told you at the beginning of this chapter, I get all kinds of questions and reactions when someone first learns about IULs and I don't take it personally. One such question is "how is this legal?" or "is this legal?"

The answer, of course, is that IULs are indeed legal. In fact, the insurance industry as a whole and, in particular, the life insurance industry is heavily regulated by federal authorities and state authorities including the SCC. Furthermore, there are rules specific to the IUL product itself – which, of course, pre-determines what a company or broker or agent is capable of offering. In short, the feds know about the IUL and so do the states.

As far as the IUL product, itself, it has been around for nearly 20 years and many of the insurance companies which offer the product have been around for over 100 years.

Agents and brokers who sell IULs, like myself, must be licensed by the state in order to assist, advise, or sell IULs. On top of that, the agent or broker must be licensed in the state a client resides in order to execute a new policy with a client in that state. So, in other words, even if you are licensed in one state, you cannot do business in the other 49 states unless you have a license in those states as well.

Additionally, the licensed agent or broker must be appointed (as in, approved) by the carrier insurance company offering an IUL product before being allowed to sell their IUL products.

Finally, the IUL policy, itself, is an official contract made between the insured and the insurance company.

Why hasn't my financial advisor mentioned this to me?

There are several reasons why you may have not heard about the IUL yet from your financial advisor.

For starters, not all financial advisors know about the IUL or feel knowledgeable enough to even comment on it, so why bring it up? And if an advisor's firm doesn't sell IULs, then naturally it won't be mentioned, either, and since most investment firms don't like to mix securities with insurance, this will typically be the case.

Furthermore, an IUL is an insurance product and, therefore, requires a specific type of insurance license to sell these types of indexed products.

Finally, the most human and obvious reason may be simply that a financial advisor's firm makes their money solely through the fees they charge for managing mutual funds and stock-based investment portfolios. Naturally, they will be inclined to encourage those types of investments. Notably, they make money whether you did or not.

The point is that simply because your financial advisor hasn't mentioned the IUL to you doesn't mean too much aside from the fact that he/she doesn't have the insurance or IUL expertise to discuss it with you. And to be totally frank with you, some people will speak about the IUL without the proper knowledge to do so. Therefore, proceed with caution when encountering anyone who arrogantly speaks dismissively about the IUL because as you can see, the IUL is a robust and beneficial financial product.

Why hasn't my employer(s) offered this to me?

Again, similar to my previous answer, most employers simply do not about the IUL yet or have had it offered to them by an IUL sales associate.

That said, more and more employers are beginning to offer IUL savings options - at the least, as a paycheck deduction option - especially as more CEOs, CFOs, HR personnel and business owners get educated on the product.

In fact, businesses are beginning to leverage the IUL for employee and executive benefit plans as a recruitment tool to secure and retain top talent by using it as part of a bonus incentive plan or employment package.

7

IUL VS...

Are you curious to see how the IUL stacks up against other popular retirement and insurance products out there?

Of course you are. And you know what? The IUL is not afraid to go toe to toe with any of these retirement/savings account heavy weights. And that's because the IUL is a real contender and a worthy champion for your financial security. So, in this chapter, I'm going to show you my scorecard using my point system, but at the end of the day, you be judge.

But for now, let's check out a few of these matchups featuring some of the key characteristics I've already discussed in this book which I believe to be critically important to one's financial security.

And to start things off, let's begin with the main event and see how the IUL stacks up against the one and only 401(k) plan -- which has sort of become the de facto retirement plan for many hard-working Americans today.

IUL VS 401(k)

	IUL	401(k)
Potential Market Upside [1]	✓	✓+
Protection of Principal [2] (Protection Against Market Downside)	✓	
Earnings Locked-In [3]	✓	
Tax-Deferred Growth [4] (Tax-Free Growth)	✓	✓
Tax-Free Access [5]	✓	
Potential **Tax-Free Income Stream** [6]	✓	
Tax-Free Death Benefit [7]	✓+	
Living Benefits [8]	✓	
Plan Versatility [9]	✓	
Scope & Simplicity of One Plan [10]	✓	

MATCH RECAP: IUL VS. 401(K)

Well, as you can see, when comparing the IUL to one of the heavy weights of retirement plans -- the 401(k), the IUL is clearly a worthy contender as it provides a litany of features that the 401(k) does not.

Both the IUL and 401(k) are able to accumulate cash or grow money via the markets. The 401(k) does this typically via stock-based portfolios that will rise and fall with markets every day. The IUL does this by using an index as a barometer and then checking on that barometer on an annual basis to see difference. If a positive change occurred (i.e., the market index grew), then your cash account within your IUL should capture a good portion of that percentage of growth depending upon how your IUL is configured. If the market receded, as in the market had a negative year, then your cash value is protected from any losses from the market.

The 401(k) does not protect your principal from market losses. The 401(k) does not provide you additional funds to support you in cases of critical, chronic, or terminal illnesses as living benefits may do for IULs. The 401(k) does not give you a pat on the back and lock-in the gains you made last year or 3 years ago... all those gains are on the table and still vulnerable to loss. If you started a 401(k) with $100 that was deducted out of your paycheck, you have $100 in your 401(k), but if you started an IUL with a $100, you would have exponentially more financial protection for you or your family.

As far as tax advantages go, the big draw of 401(k)s is that you are able to grow your money tax-deferred by using pre-tax money from a paycheck which is typically tax-deductible. You, therefore, are choosing to not pay taxes now on that seed money and electing to pay those taxes later on the harvest. As an example, if your paycheck was $2000 and you invested $200 of that into a company 401(k) plan, then you would only pay taxes on $1800. Meanwhile, that $200 will theoretically grow for the next 20-40 years and when you are in your 60's and it's time to tap into that money, that's the point you will pay taxes on that $200. HOWEVER, and this is a big HOWEVER, you need to realize that you are paying the taxes on whatever amount that $200 grew to be which clearly is probably going to be a much bigger number many years in the future. Keep in mind, of course, you are not just funding a 401(k) with a single contribution of $200, but rather, with a stream of contributions over many years.

With an IUL, on the other hand, you are using post-tax money to fund it which is what fundamentally allows the tax-free access. So, in this case, you would receive your paycheck as you normally would with all of its standard federal, state, and local deductions, but in this case, you will use your "take-home pay" or "after-tax" money to fund the IUL. In other words, you are paying taxes on the seed now so you can have a tax-free harvest later.

Do 401(k)s ever make sense to do?

After looking at *my versus chart* and understanding it, you may wonder if 401(k)s are ever a good idea. And the answer is yes, sometimes, it is and it's wise to take advantage of them. For example, if your contributions to your company 401(k) plan are being matched by the company 1:1, then that would be a worthy reason to keep investing in it while you have that matching because that's free money which is essentially doubling your contribution. That said, even in that scenario, there are "contribution limits" to be aware of. And even then, that doesn't change the facts about the risk your money is probably exposed to or, perhaps, the need for additional products to match the spectrum of benefits that an IUL does provide. Ultimately, these decisions are between you and the financial professionals you work with.

But what if you lose or leave your job? What if your next workplace doesn't offer any 401(k) matching? Do you still want to invest in it like you were? Do you still want to pay taxes later on the harvest rather than paying the tax on the seed now? These answers might just boil down to personal preference as to whether you want to pay taxes now or later.

Finally, with regards to the cost of these plans, the short - answer on that is that 401k) plans typically have what's called "management fees" attached to them which typically range from 1-3% of your principal. This includes any recordkeeping and admin work which is done to maintain the account. The cost of an IUL essentially boils down to the cost of insurance which is included within your premium amount and is based, in large part, on your age.

"*Ouch! That Downside Protection hit hard.*"

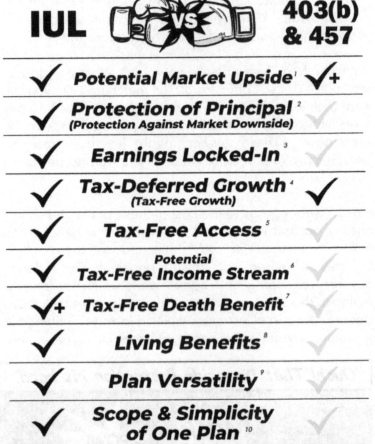

IUL VS **403(b) & 457**

	IUL	403(b) & 457
Potential Market Upside [1]	✓	✓+
Protection of Principal [2] (Protection Against Market Downside)	✓	
Earnings Locked-In [3]	✓	
Tax-Deferred Growth [4] (Tax-Free Growth)	✓	✓
Tax-Free Access [5]	✓	
Potential **Tax-Free Income Stream** [6]	✓	
Tax-Free Death Benefit [7]	✓+	
Living Benefits [8]	✓	
Plan Versatility [9]	✓	
Scope & Simplicity of One Plan [10]	✓	

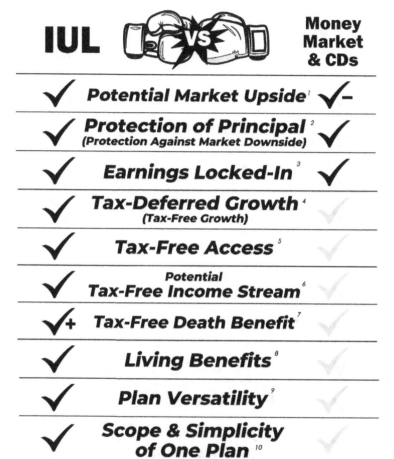

IUL vs **Money Market & CDs**

IUL		Money Market & CDs
✓	**Potential Market Upside**[1]	✓–
✓	**Protection of Principal**[2] (Protection Against Market Downside)	✓
✓	**Earnings Locked-In**[3]	✓
✓	**Tax-Deferred Growth**[4] (Tax-Free Growth)	✓
✓	**Tax-Free Access**[5]	
✓	Potential **Tax-Free Income Stream**[6]	
✓+	**Tax-Free Death Benefit**[7]	
✓	**Living Benefits**[8]	
✓	**Plan Versatility**[9]	
✓	**Scope & Simplicity of One Plan**[10]	

For educational purposes only, subject to changes in state and/or federal laws. Not a recommendation for or against any particular type of plan. 1. Potential cash accumulation based on positive performance of financial market(s). IUL typically based upon annual basis. 2. Principal considered to be cash values in account. IUL typically has 0 floor. 3. For IUL, each year credited gains (if any) are permanently added to principal and reset for subsequent year 4. Cash accumulation growing tax-free due to tax-deferred basis. 5. Cash values may be distributed/withdrawn tax-free. IUL may be accessed tax-free via a policy loan provision if structured properly. If done as straight withdrawal (or if policy lapses) there will be tax liability for IUL. 6. A tax-free supplemental income stream may be available if cash values in account reach minimal distribution thresholds and if structured properly per account/policy stipulations and limitations 7. Cash value in account distributed to beneficiaries tax-free. Insurance policies typically have pre-determined value allocated for death benefit regardless of cash accumulated values. 8. Access to insurance death benefit for critical, chronic, or terminal illnesses as defined per the policy contract. Living benefit withdrawals reduce death benefit. 9. IUL policies are highly versatile with customizable provisions, premiums, tax advantages and potential adaptations throughout the lifetime of the policy. 10. IUL typically provides all of the features of this chart with one policy plan or account, but variations and limitations may exist by carrier. Copyright 2021 IULASAP.com

IUL	VS	Traditional IRA
✓	**Potential Market Upside** [1]	✓+
✓	**Protection of Principal** [2] **(Protection Against Market Downside)**	
✓	**Earnings Locked-In** [3]	
✓	**Tax-Deferred Growth** [4] **(Tax-Free Growth)**	✓
✓	**Tax-Free Access** [5]	
✓	**Potential Tax-Free Income Stream** [6]	
✓+	**Tax-Free Death Benefit** [7]	
✓	**Living Benefits** [8]	
✓	**Plan Versatility** [9]	
✓	**Scope & Simplicity of One Plan** [10]	

IUL VS **Traditional ROTH IRA**

	IUL		Traditional ROTH IRA
Potential Market Upside [1]	✓		✓ +
Protection of Principal [2] (Protection Against Market Downside)	✓		
Earnings Locked-In [3]	✓		
Tax-Deferred Growth [4] (Tax-Free Growth)	✓		✓
Tax-Free Access [5]	✓		✓
Potential **Tax-Free Income Stream** [6]	✓		
Tax-Free Death Benefit [7]	✓ +		✓
Living Benefits [8]	✓		
Plan Versatility [9]	✓		
Scope & Simplicity of One Plan [10]	✓		

For educational purposes only, subject to changes in state and/or federal laws. Not a recommendation for or against any particular type of plan. 1. Potential cash accumulation based on positive performance of financial market(s). IUL typically based upon annual basis. 2. Principal considered to be cash values in account. IUL typically has 0 floor. 3. For IUL, each year credited gains (if any) are permanently added to principal and reset for subsequent year 4. Cash accumulation growing tax-free due to tax-deferred basis. 5. Cash values may be distributed/withdrawn tax-free. IUL may be accessed tax-free via a policy loan provision if structured properly. If done as straight withdrawal (or if policy lapses) there will be tax liability for IUL. 6. A tax-free supplemental income stream may be available if cash values in account reach minimal distribution thresholds and if structured properly per account/policy stipulations and limitations 7. Cash value in account distributed to beneficiaries tax-free. Insurance policies typically have pre-determined value allocated for death benefit regardless of cash accumulated values. 8. Access to insurance death benefit for critical, chronic, or terminal illnesses as defined per the policy contract. Living benefit withdrawals reduce death benefit. 9. IUL policies are highly versatile with customizable provisions, premiums, tax advantages and potential adaptations throughout the lifetime of the policy. 10. IUL typically provides all of the features of this chart with one policy plan or account, but variations and limitations may exist by carrier. Copyright 2021 IULASAP.com

IUL **VS** TSP

IUL		TSP
✓	**Potential Market Upside** [1]	✓+
✓	**Protection of Principal** [2] (Protection Against Market Downside)	✓
✓	**Earnings Locked-In** [3]	✓
✓	**Tax-Deferred Growth** [4] (Tax-Free Growth)	✓
✓	**Tax-Free Access** [5]	✓
✓	Potential **Tax-Free Income Stream** [6]	✓
✓+	**Tax-Free Death Benefit** [7]	✓
✓	**Living Benefits** [8]	✓
✓	**Plan Versatility** [9]	✓
✓	**Scope & Simplicity of One Plan** [10]	✓

For educational purposes only, subject to changes in state and/or federal laws. Not a recommendation for or against any particular type of plan. 1. Potential cash accumulation based on positive performance of financial market(s). IUL typically based upon annual basis. 2. Principal considered to be cash values in account. IUL typically has 0 floor. 3. For IUL, each year credited gains (if any) are permanently added to principal and reset for subsequent year 4. Cash accumulation growing tax-free due to tax-deferred basis. 5. Cash values may be distributed/withdrawn tax-free. IUL may be accessed tax-free via a policy loan provision if structured properly. If done as straight withdrawal (or if policy lapses) there will be tax liability for IUL. 6. A tax-free supplemental income stream may be available if cash values in account reach minimal distribution thresholds and if structured properly per account/policy stipulations and limitations 7. Cash value in account distributed to beneficiaries tax-free. Insurance policies typically have pre-determined value allocated for death benefit regardless of cash accumulated values. 8. Access to insurance death benefit for critical, chronic, or terminal illnesses as defined per the policy contract. Living benefit withdrawals reduce death benefit. 9. IUL policies are highly versatile with customizable provisions, premiums, tax advantages and potential adaptations throughout the lifetime of the policy. 10. IUL typically provides all of the features of this chart with one policy plan or account, but variations and limitations may exist by carrier. Copyright 2021 IULASAP.com

IUL vs **WHOLE LIFE**

IUL	Feature	WHOLE LIFE
✓	**Potential Market Upside**[1]	
✓	**Protection of Principal**[2] (Protection Against Market Downside)	✓
✓	**Earnings Locked-In**[3]	✓
✓	**Tax-Deferred Growth**[4] (Tax-Free Growth)	✓
✓	**Tax-Free Access**[5]	✓
✓	Potential **Tax-Free Income Stream**[6]	✓
✓+	**Tax-Free Death Benefit**[7]	✓
✓	**Living Benefits**[8]	✓
✓	**Plan Versatility**[9]	
✓	**Scope & Simplicity of One Plan**[10]	

For educational purposes only, subject to changes in state and/or federal laws. Not a recommendation for or against any particular type of plan. 1. Potential cash accumulation based on positive performance of financial market(s). IUL typically based upon annual basis. 2. Principal considered to be cash values in account. IUL typically has 0 floor. 3. For IUL, each year credited gains (if any) are permanently added to principal and reset for subsequent year 4. Cash accumulation growing tax-free due to tax-deferred basis. 5. Cash values may be distributed/withdrawn tax-free. IUL may be accessed tax-free via a policy loan provision if structured properly. If done as straight withdrawal (or if policy lapses) there will be tax liability for IUL. 6. A tax-free supplemental income stream may be available if cash values in account reach minimal distribution thresholds and if structured properly per account/policy stipulations and limitations 7. Cash value in account distributed to beneficiaries tax-free. Insurance policies typically have pre-determined value allocated for death benefit regardless of cash accumulated values. 8. Access to insurance death benefit for critical, chronic, or terminal illnesses as defined per the policy contract. Living benefit withdrawals reduce death benefit. 9. IUL policies are highly versatile with customizable provisions, premiums, tax advantages and potential adaptations throughout the lifetime of the policy. 10. IUL typically provides all of the features of this chart with one policy plan or account, but variations and limitations may exist   by carrier. Copyright 2021 IULASAP.com

IUL vs **VARIABLE LIFE**

IUL		VARIABLE LIFE
✓	**Potential Market Upside**[1]	✓+
✓	**Protection of Principal**[2] (Protection Against Market Downside)	✓
✓	**Earnings Locked-In**[3]	✓
✓	**Tax-Deferred Growth**[4] (Tax-Free Growth)	✓
✓	**Tax-Free Access**[5]	✓
✓	Potential **Tax-Free Income Stream**[6]	✓
✓+	**Tax-Free Death Benefit**[7]	✓
✓	**Living Benefits**[8]	✓
✓	**Plan Versatility**[9]	✓
✓	**Scope & Simplicity of One Plan**[10]	✓

For educational purposes only, subject to changes in state and/or federal laws. Not a recommendation for or against any particular type of plan. 1. Potential cash accumulation based on positive performance of financial market(s). IUL typically based upon annual basis. 2. Principal considered to be cash values in account. IUL typically has 0 floor. 3. For IUL, each year credited gains (if any) are permanently added to principal and reset for subsequent year 4. Cash accumulation growing tax-free due to tax-deferred basis. 5. Cash values may be distributed/withdrawn tax-free. IUL may be accessed tax-free via a policy loan provision if structured properly. If done as straight withdrawal (or if policy lapses) there will be tax liability for IUL. 6. A tax-free supplemental income stream may be available if cash values in account reach minimal distribution thresholds and if structured properly per account/policy stipulations and limitations 7. Cash value in account distributed to beneficiaries tax-free. Insurance policies typically have pre-determined value allocated for death benefit regardless of cash accumulated values. 8. Access to insurance death benefit for critical, chronic, or terminal illnesses as defined per the policy contract. Living benefit withdrawals reduce death benefit. 9. IUL policies are highly versatile with customizable provisions, premiums, tax advantages and potential adaptations throughout the lifetime of the policy. 10. IUL typically provides all of the features of this chart with one policy plan or account, but variations and limitations may exist by carrier. Copyright 2021 IULASAP.com

IUL vs **TERM LIFE**

IUL		TERM LIFE
✓	**Potential Market Upside**[1]	✓
✓	**Protection of Principal**[2] **(Protection Against Market Downside)**	✓
✓	**Earnings Locked-In**[3]	
✓	**Tax-Deferred Growth**[4] **(Tax-Free Growth)**	
✓	**Tax-Free Access**[5]	
✓	**Potential** **Tax-Free Income Stream**[6]	
✓+	**Tax-Free Death Benefit**[7]	✓
✓	**Living Benefits**[8]	✓
✓	**Plan Versatility**[9]	
✓	**Scope & Simplicity** **of One Plan**[10]	

For educational purposes only, subject to changes in state and/or federal laws. Not a recommendation for or against any particular type of plan. 1. Potential cash accumulation based on positive performance of financial market(s). IUL typically based upon annual basis. 2. Principal considered to be cash values in account. IUL typically has 0 floor. 3. For IUL, each year credited gains (if any) are permanently added to principal and reset for subsequent year 4. Cash accumulation growing tax-free due to tax-deferred basis. 5. Cash values may be distributed/withdrawn tax-free. IUL may be accessed tax-free via a policy loan provision if structured properly. If done as straight withdrawal (or if policy lapses) there will be tax liability for IUL. 6. A tax-free supplemental income stream may be available if cash values in account reach minimal distribution thresholds and if structured properly per account/policy stipulations and limitations 7. Cash value in account distributed to beneficiaries tax-free. Insurance policies typically have pre-determined value allocated for death benefit regardless of cash accumulated values. 8. Access to insurance death benefit for critical, chronic, or terminal illnesses as defined per the policy contract. Living benefit withdrawals reduce death benefit. 9. IUL policies are highly versatile with customizable provisions, premiums, tax advantages and potential adaptations throughout the lifetime of the policy. 10. IUL typically provides all of the features of this chart with one policy plan or account, but variations and limitations may exist by carrier. Copyright 2021 IULASAP.com

MATCH RECAP: IUL VS. THE REST

Rather than repeat myself over and over again, here's my recap for IUL vs. the rest of the pack I feature here.

Money Market Accounts and ***CDs*** (Certificates of Deposit) are typically low-risk very low-yield investments. You are protected against the downside, but the upside is minimal and limited. With an IUL, you can capture much more of the upside while also having the financial security of death and living benefits.

Traditional IRAs, 403(b), 457, TSP, and 401(k) plans are all considered tax-advantaged retirement accounts that enable your money to grow tax-deferred, but considering those funds are all invested into the financial markets, that means they will all face similar market risk exposure (and therefore may decrease due to market losses or recessions) AND will depend on the performance of whatever fund managers are actively optimizing those accounts. On the other hand, with an IUL, you have indexed cash accumulation which means your money will grow with the market by using the index values and crediting your cash account accordingly based on configuration and structure of your IUL.

With a ***Traditional ROTH IRA***, post-tax investment grows money tax-free and tax-free distribution (access) is available after, usually, 5 years of participation. Money is in the market and therefore may still suffer losses. With an IUL, you are able to grow your money tax-free and you have tax-free access so it behaves similarly in that fashion. The IUL grows money leveraging market performance as well, but because your IUL cash values are not technically in the market, an IUL is able to protect your principal from the downside and, therefore, will not suffer any losses due to market losses, crashes, or recessions.

Notably, none of these traditional accounts allow for an annual reset that locks in whatever gains were possibly made in the preceding year. The IUL does have such a provision which ratchets up your protected principal each and every year your account is credited with gains based on market growth.

Term Insurance is the closest thing to pure life insurance meaning its primary focus is solely to provide a death benefit, but that protection is temporary. Only if the insured dies during the term or period of coverage will a death benefit be paid. An IUL, on the other hand, is permanent life insurance so assuming your policy is in force, the protection will last your entire life and a death benefit will definitely be paid at some point. Some term plans offer living benefits which is why I checked off living benefits, but many if not most do not, so keep that in mind. With term life insurance, there is no cash value or cash accumulation or potential supplemental income.

Whole life is a cash-value based life insurance account that typically offers fixed rates of return around 4%.

Variable universal life insurance typically allows for full capture of market upside, but it will not protect your principal and it will not reset your gains every year.

With regards to **tax-deferred accounts,** as I mentioned in chapter 5, the general notion is that when you retire you will be in a lower tax-bracket because you will be making less income -- and therefore pay a lower rate of taxes when you begin to receive money from your tax-deferred accounts. However, as many financial analysts will point out, this assumption is becoming more questionable since many people continue to earn money beyond 65 years during their so-called "retirement years." Also, this assumption is betting, in part, that taxes will not increase in the future which many people would think to be a risky proposition.

On the other hand, with an IUL, yes it, too, grows with a tax-deferred status, but since you are funding it with post-tax money and because of the existence of the special IUL policy loan feature which essentially enables you to access your cash value tax-free, you do not have to worry about what the taxes will be like in the future. Many people, including myself, would consider that a positive.

Finally, please keep in mind that despite how lob-sided these matchups may look, I'm not saying that any or all of these other types of financial accounts don't have a place in your financial portfolio. Again, at the end of the day you and the financial professionals you work with will need to be the judge.

That said, if the features I've chosen for the sake of the comparison in this chapter are valuable to you, then perhaps it may suit you to consult with an IUL agent and request an illustration so you can see for yourself how an IUL may work for you.

8

A.S.A.P.

By now, you should have a pretty good understanding of the IUL. In fact, if you have digested the entire book so far and understood it, you probably know more about the IUL than a large majority of the American population.

What you choose to do from here, of course, is your decision. Logically, if you read this book, you are already, perhaps, considering the IUL for yourself, your family, or your business.

So, what's the next step?

The answer is if you want to learn more or really see for yourself what an IUL could potentially do for you, **the next step would be to find a licensed IUL agent and request a personalized illustration.**

Which brings me to the title of this chapter and the word that is in the title of this book: A.S.A.P.

Yes, ASAP means AS SOON AS POSSIBLE, but what do I mean exactly?

Well, to be clear, when I say IUL ASAP, first of all, I don't mean, "get an IUL as soon as possible." I cannot advise you to do anything with IULs or anything else until I have a meeting with you and exchange some information so that I can make a suitable recommendation based on your best interests and needs.

What I do mean by "IUL ASAP," is that you need to know about this product AS SOON AS POSSIBLE. Why? Because what if an IUL is a perfect fit for you and your financial security? Wouldn't you want to know that AS SOON AS POSSIBLE? Of course you would.

But there's another meaning to the use of ASAP, especially as it relates to this chapter. ASAP is a word we use to signal urgency, right? It's a matter of TIME, right? And as it turns out, MONEY and TIME are very closely related when it comes to the financial game of life.

So with that being said, let me offer you some what-if scenarios to consider as you ponder your next step.

1. What if the market crashed?

It's been a great few years recently, as far as the financial markets are concerned, but there's also no denying that as I write this book, the markets are a little shaky as the economy continues to strive for normalcy amidst heavy government spending and early signs of inflation.

So, it's worth asking what if the market crashed? What would be the impact for you? More specifically, do you have any retirement accounts invested in the stock market? Any mutual funds? 401(k) plans? IRAs?

If so, you may want to re-evaluate the market risk your accounts may be currently exposed to -- and affirm for yourself if you are comfortable with that exposure in what has truly become a new world that seems filled with uncertainty and global turmoil.

No doubt the US financial markets have remained incredibly resilient during the global pandemic, but will that always be the case?

These are worthy questions to consider ASAP.

An IUL, as you now know, would protect you from a market crash or any significant economic downturn as far as the financial markets are concerned. Worst case scenario is that your IUL has a zero year, and that could potentially be a great thing.

2. What if the market spiked?

What if the market finished strong and had another great year this year? Or next year? Wouldn't you want to capture that market upside?

Are you content with your money in your checking/savings account earning less than 1%? Actually, last time I checked, it was even less than a tenth of 1%! [14]

Are you content having money lose value due to inflation with nothing to offset it? Because chances are that in a year of significant market growth, your IUL would capture a good portion of the upside.

---

[14] Stephanie Vozza "Average Bank Interest Rates in 2021: Checking, Savings and Money Market Rates" valuepenguin.com (accessed May 24, 2021)

3. What if your health gets worse in the future?

Nobody likes to contemplate their own demise, I get it, but that shouldn't get in the way of wisdom and commonsense, either.

So let me ask you a question. What if your health got significantly worse sometime in the future? Is that possible? Would you be prepared financially? What if your life depended on it? What if you suffered a bad accident? What if you were diagnosed with a critical, chronic, or terminal illness?

With an IUL, at least you would potentially have access to your death benefit money WHILE STILL ALIVE via the living benefits provisions if your condition was serious enough to qualify you for them.

In that case, you would potentially have access to 6 or 7 figures of cash to use when you need it most. That's especially powerful when you consider the leveraged benefits that you walk away from the table upon securing an IUL.

On the flipside, let's say someone had his/her first $200 set aside from their paycheck to invest into a 401(k) company plan or simply invested their first $200 into an IRA. Then, that someone became critically, chronically, or terminally ill (and to the same degree that would have qualified for living benefits from an IUL). In the end, that person would still only have $200.

At the end of the day, living benefits translates to additional financial protections against severe health

downturns that would otherwise potentially bankrupt you or perhaps force you to accept lower standards of health care.

4. What if taxes increase?

If you currently possess a traditional IRA, 401(k), or other tax-deferred account, the assumption is that taxes will be less when you reach retirement age. But people are not retiring like they used to. Now people retire into new lines of work -- often still earning significant incomes through their 60s and well into their 70s. This results in the assumption of a low-tax tax-advantage for tax-deferred accounts to be more questionable than ever before.

Furthermore, what if taxes are simply much higher overall when you begin to withdraw money from your tax-deferred account? What if every tax bracket has been increased? This, too, may chip away at that tax advantage of the tax-deferred account. There is no way to know for certain until you get to the point of distribution. And as I mentioned earlier in the book, tax brackets have historically been much higher than they currently are now and who is to say that isn't possible again - especially with all of the government spending we are seeing recently.

With an IUL, while it too is able to accumulate cash on a tax-deferred basis and therefore benefit from tax-free growth, the difference is that you are able to, practically speaking, access it tax-free via the policy loan provision.

5. What if the laws changed?

The laws that govern the tax treatment of insurance

products or the products themselves sometimes change. This doesn't happen often, but it definitely happens.

In fact, many years ago in the 1980s, laws had to be created for life insurance products, in particular, because many rich and wise people took advantage of the tax-free tax advantages of life insurance to the point that it seemed abusive.

People were essentially stuffing their life insurance policies with large amounts of cash value while acquiring low levels of life insurance (death benefit). This forced the government to eventually create specific MEC ratios that essentially forced the death benefit to be somewhat proportional to the cash value within a policy.

Specifically, **IRS code section 7702** is the part of the tax code that defines life insurance and the various limitations, MEC definitions and any parameters that the policies must stay within in order to sustain tax advantages. [15]

An IUL policy owner doesn't want their IUL to become a MEC (Modified Endowment Contract) because the tax-deferred status and tax-free access would then be compromised and taxes would be owed.

But not only that, as I was writing this book, the laws changed again in December of 2020. Again, the last time there was a significant change, it was in the 1980s. In large part, these new 2020 updates to section 7702 affect whole life insurance and universal life, including IULs.

And here's the short story on what changed with regards to the IUL, in particular: premium limits were increased.

---

[15] IRS "Section 7702.—Life Insurance Contract Defined" irs.gov (accessed May 24, 2021)

So, basically, you will be able to invest more premium than before for a particular death benefit amount. The effect is that IULs will become even more suitable for cash accumulation strategies than before.

Conversely, looking at the IUL premium limits law change from a death benefit focused point-of-view, you are getting less death benefit based on the same premium amount. But again, the net effect is that the IUL remains an even stronger retirement/savings tool. Furthermore, if you wanted more death benefit, there are also ways to integrate term insurance into your IUL plan design to boost the DB if desired.

Therefore, I would say that it seems that the new 7702 changes will only make the IULs stronger in my opinion. That said, what if the laws changed again, but for the worse?

Well, the good news is that as far as I know, when laws do change in relation to insurance or life insurance, they apply for future policies only. In other words, people who purchased policies according to a particular set of rules are usually "grandfathered" into those rules for the lifetime of their policy and don't have to worry about the changes.

That said, this is yet another reason to consider "getting in" ASAP.

6. What if you died tomorrow?

Don't get uncomfortable. I'll make this short and sweet and a matter of fact.

If you were to pass away, what would be the consequence

of that to your loved ones, financially speaking? In other words, is your family protected? Or your spouse? Or your children? Would you leave a legacy behind?

When it comes to the financial game of life, especially as it relates to death, this is where the rich really know how to play the game. The rich know how to preserve wealth and create wealth at the same time. The rich use life insurance as one of their main tools to accomplish this.

And that's why it's healthy to contemplate death from a matter-of-fact point of view. You don't have to be emotional or fearful about it. Just be practical and prudent. No matter what, don't ignore it.

7. What if you wait?

What if you simply waited to move forward? What if you simply procrastinated proactive action toward savings or retirement planning?

Well, as I mentioned at the beginning of this chapter, MONEY and TIME are closely related.

So, regardless of those other what-if scenarios I just spoke of, let's look at what would definitely happen if you decided to wait, even just one year.

And, in particular, let's just focus on the IUL for now...

The IUL cost of insurance increases with age.

When you are young and in your 20s, cost of insurance will be low. When you are in your 50s, cost of insurance will be much higher. The higher your cost of insurance, the lower your cash contribution is per premium payment.

It will take more money to reach a desired supplemental income stream amount with every passing year.

If you get an IUL illustration at age 45, you will see the numbers illustrated for you at that age. You will see how much money you have to invest via premiums to reach your desired outcome.

If you wait one year and get an IUL illustration at age 46, you will notice that your minimum premium amount is slightly more and that the supplemental income that is potentially available (at the illustrated rate) is slightly less.

With every passing year, this pattern holds true which means, for example, if you desire a specific supplemental income stream amount for retirement, you will have to commit to a higher premium to do so.

I can hear you now. "But that's just one year's difference! How can that be?"

The answer is because of the magic of compound interest. And just as compound interest can excite you, it can depress you, too, if you ignore it and don't leverage it.

In fact, Albert Einstein once said that "***compound interest is the eighth wonder of the world. He who understands it, earns it ... he who doesn't ... pays it.***" [16]

Not surprisingly, that's a genius way to look at it, but check out this chart that follows and I think it will say it all.

---

[16] GoodReads "Albert Einstein Quotable Quotes" goodreads.com (accessed May 24, 2021)

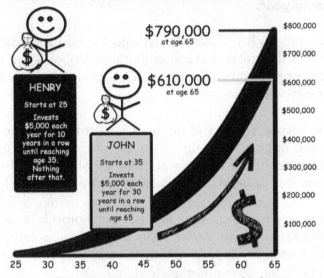

THE POWER OF STARTING EARLIER*

$790,000 at age 65

$610,000 at age 65

HENRY

Starts at 25

Invests $5,000 each year for 10 years in a row until reaching age 35. Nothing after that.

JOHN

Starts at 35

Invests $5,000 each year for 30 years in a row until reaching age 65

$800,000
$700,000
$600,000
$500,000
$400,000
$300,000
$200,000
$100,000

25 30 35 40 45 50 55 60 65

* Assumes 8 % interest rate, compounded annually. Approximates values shown.

© IULASAP.com

Notice how 25-year-old Henry invested for only 10 years (totaling $50,000) and then invested nothing after that. AND YET, Henry was still able to accumulate more money than John, even though John invested for 3x as long (30 years) and 3x as much ($150,000).

In short, the sooner you save, the easier it is for your money to grow exponentially to a larger amount, when compared to someone who starts 10 years later and saves for 2x to 3x more... all because of the magic of compound interest. As Einstein says, you either pay it or earn it, so make every year count!

FINAL WORD

I sincerely hope that you found this book informative, helpful, honest, and empowering.

My purpose was to inform you about one of the most robust financial products you may have never heard about. If your financial security is strengthened in any way because of what you read here, then I have truly achieved my purpose and I bid you good fortune.

I also hope that based on what you now know, some of you may realize that the IUL is a serious contender to be a champion for your financial security.

In that case, I encourage you to take the next step. I encourage you to speak with an IUL agent and get a look at it for yourself.

And if you don't happen to have someone to help you along the way, then I would be happy to help you navigate the next steps toward your financial security.

I am also giving special priority to the readers of my book if you reach me here: ***https://iulasap.com/freeconsult***

BONUS CHAPTER 9

THERE IS ANOTHER WAY

As I illustrated with my hierarchy of needs infographic, income is fundamentally important to your financial security which is why it rests on the bottom of the triangle – it represents the foundation. Income is like food and water in terms of basic financial survival.

This is why one of the main reasons why I love the IUL as a worthy product of consideration is for its potential tax-free supplemental income stream. Keep in mind, naturally, this income stream does not become provisionally available to you until your cash value within your IUL reaches a certain point or threshold and if structured properly. You can see when this supplemental income would hypothetically become available to you with an IUL illustration.

But what if you already had a considerable amount of money accumulated and saved up somewhere or sitting in one or more of your investment accounts?

Well then, in that case, **there is another way.**

In other words, there is another financial product that would address several financial security needs (like the IUL) while featuring guaranteed income for life.

Like the IUL, it's another insurance product (meaning the insurance companies created it), but in this case, we're not talking life insurance of any kind - so no medical underwriting ever because medical info is irrelevant.

Like the IUL, it's also an indexed product which allows your money to continue to grow by using the financial markets as a barometer for that growth.

Like the IUL, your principal has a zero-floor and, therefore, offers true downside protection since your account cannot decrease due to market losses or downturns.

And like the IUL, there is typically an annual reset provision of some kind which locks in your credited gains of the past year if there were any.

But unlike the IUL, because these accounts require minimal deposit amounts to begin with, the supplemental income stream is guaranteed from day one and the income stream will last until the day you die. In other words, you are transforming money into money you cannot outlive - and it is a certainty from day one.

As you may have already guessed by now, I am referring to the breed of products known as annuities, but the kind I'm speaking of in particular is a special class of annuities.

To read the rest of the chapter and learn exactly what this other 3-letter word is as well as receive a special gift from me (Shirley), simply visit the link below:

https://iulasap.com/anotherway

BONUS CHAPTER 10

THE 5-YEAR RETIREMENT PLAN

As you now know, I consider the concept of leverage – specifically, the ability to leverage financial products to further one's financial security – as one of the top secrets to winning the financial game of life.

And if you were a good student digesting this book, you should also know by now that the IUL is a powerful product in terms of its ability to address multiple financial security needs with a single account. It leverages the cash accumulating forces of nature while protecting you against various risks and losses as well. I've also highlighted 12 specific reasons why you should consider the IUL as a potential cornerstone for your financial security needs.

But what if I told you that not only can the IUL do the leveraging, but that the IUL, itself, can be leveraged? And in such a way to as to provide you a robust retirement plan that only required 5 years of contributions from you? Actually, to be more specific it would only require five premium contributions once a year. Would you be interested in that?

I call it the 5-Year Retirement Plan.

But what if I told you one more thing... that this 5-year retirement plan would give you match contribution 3 to 1 for every dollar you put in, would you be interested in that?

The truth is you would be crazy not to be.

Once you realize that I'm not crazy and you allow the reality of what I just said to sink in - as you realize that not only can you acquire a product that has all of the features, benefits, and potential options of an IUL, but that you can also leverage 3 dollars for every 1 dollar you put in - honestly, at that point, you should feel nothing short of shock and awe.

As I said earlier, the secret to winning the financial game of life is to leverage money, but here's another part to that secret - and it's this: whenever possible leverage other people's money. This allows your cash flow to be minimally affected while theoretically still reaping the benefits from the investment.

That's how the super-rich like to play the game, but the great news is you don't have to be super rich to qualify for the 5-year retirement plan. In fact, if your combined household income is $100,000 or greater, then this is a plan you may be able to consider.

But let's not forget the part that people really love... and that's the potential for a TAX-FREE SUPPLEMENTAL INCOME STREAM (when properly structured). Because of the unique 3:1 leverage of this plan design, that means you are able to generate a much higher than normal tax-free supplemental income stream. You could call it an IUL on steroids, but in this case, there are no side effects - except for higher monetary death benefit protection for you and your loved ones, a bigger potential pot of money for living benefits if you need it, and a potential income stream that looks like a nice pension plan, TAX-FREE.

To read the rest of this chapter or to learn more about this 5-year retirement plan, simply visit the online URL below and insert your age to see what this plan could potentially do for you.

https://IULASAP.com/5yearplan

ACKNOWLEDGEMENTS

First of all, I owe an enormous debt of gratitude to my editor Enzo Giovanni who not only edited my book, but has served as the master architect for the entire book project online and offline. His insight is priceless as was his patience for all of my corrections! His ability to extract the best out of people is a marvel to behold and I will forever cherish this experience.

Thank you to all of those clients, business partners, and countless media platforms who contributed to help spread the message to all that we serve about the importance of financial literacy.

I would like to express a special thanks full of gratitude to Debbie and Phil Gerlicher who gave me a "golden opportunity" many years ago and have helped me develop my leadership skills along the way.

To Ron and Liz Wheeler, thank you for always making me feel special enough that I can take on the world.

To all of the folks at in Atlanta who are the unsung heroes for so much of the work that I do.

To all my colleagues, teammates and top-notch carriers such as *American Equity*, *American National Insurance Company*, *National Life Group*, and *North American* for the support that has provided a platform for me to thrive in a competitive world of finance and enabled me to achieve this level of success.

Thank you to my social media support team, to my admin team in Virginia for helping to promote my brand name, and to my client support team which has allowed me to focus on making this book happen.

To all of my kids who provide unconditional love, thank you.

Finally, I want to thank my better half, Hoang Vu, who provides constant support and tolerates my incessant disappearances into my work while also helping me to manage our household and keeping me grounded as a parent at the same time. A lifelong partner makes both the journey and destination worthwhile.

ONLINE RESOURCE LINKS

Find an IUL Broker Agent
https://iulasap.com/agent

IUL Info for Churches & Non-Profit Organizations
https://iulasap.com/mission

IUL Info for Businesses and Corporations
https://iulasap.com/business

Free IUL Consult with Shirley Luu
https://iulasap.com/freeconsult

Bonus Chapter for "Another Way"
https://iulasap.com/anotherway

Bonus Chapter for "The 5-Year Plan"
https://IULASAP.com/5yearplan

Financial Services Career/Job Information
https://iulasap.com/careers

ABOUT SHIRLEY LUU

Shirley Luu is an award-winning financial consultant, hands-on-trainer, author, national speaker on financial literacy, and renown "*wealth guru*." Her 25 years of experience in the financial services and insurance field as one of the industry's top producers and trainers sets her apart as one of the industry's most knowledgeable experts.

Shirley Luu has earned numerous awards, locally and nationally. These recognitions stem from her proven success and quality service in business, her support for non-profit and philanthropic causes, and for her excellence in leadership by virtue of the thousands of people she has trained and coached in the field. Shirley Luu also continues to be a steadfast champion and advocate for the empowerment of minorities and women with her financial literacy programs, entrepreneurship opportunities, and advanced wealth concepts training.

Shirley Luu has been a featured guest or topic on various TV and Radio networks and publications such as ABC, CBS, FOX, Sirius XM, Forbes and Oprah Magazine.

Shirley Luu is the founder and CEO of Shirley Luu & Associates, LLC – a financial brokerage firm specializing in insurance and annuity products. She also serves as the Executive Field Chairman for First Financial Security, Inc.

INCOME & CAREERS

If you are interested in a career in financial services or in applying for a position in Shirley Luu's organization (which does business across the country in all 50 states), then visit **https://iulasap.com/careers** for more information.

MONEY MAKEOVERS & WEALTH EDUCATION WITH SHIRLEY LUU

Shirley Luu provides various empowering wealth-education based programs dealing with personal finance, success, and entrepreneurship.

To see what programs are currently available, visit **https://iulasap.com/360**

Made in United States
Orlando, FL
27 June 2024

48353271R00098